The Actor in You

FOURTH EDITION

The Actor in You

Sixteen Simple Steps to Understanding the Art of Acting

Robert Benedetti

Boston ■ New York ■ San Francisco

Mexico City ■ Montreal ■ Toronto ■ London ■ Madrid ■ Munich ■ Paris

Hong Kong ■ Singapore ■ Tokyo ■ Cape Town ■ Sydney

Acquisitions Editor: *Jeanne Zalesky*
Editorial Assistant: *Brian Mickelson*
Marketing Manager: *Suzan Czajkowski*
Senior Production Administrator: *Donna Simons*
Composition Buyer: *Linda Cox*
Cover Administrator: *Kristina Mose-Libon*
Manufacturing Buyer: *JoAnne Sweeney*
Editorial-Production Service: *Erin Melloy, S4Carlisle Publishing Services*
Electronic Composition: *S4Carlisle Publishing Services*

For related titles and support materials, visit our online catalog at www.ablongman.com.

Between the time website information is gathered and then published, it is not unusual for some sites to have closed. Also, the transcription of URLs can result in typographical errors. The publisher would appreciate notification where these errors occur so they may be corrected in subsequent editions.

Library of Congress Cataloging-in-Publication Data

Benedetti, Robert.
 The actor in you : sixteen simple steps to understanding the art of acting / Robert Benedetti.— 4th ed.
  p. cm.
 Includes bibliographical references and index.
 ISBN 0-205-54208-5
 I. Title.

PN2061.B392 2009
792.02′8—dc22   2007034604

Printed in the United States of America

10   9   8   7   6   5   4   3   2   1   11   10   09   08   07

CONTENTS

NOTES ON THIS FOURTH EDITION

My first acting book, *The Actor at Work*, was written forty years ago and is about to enter its tenth edition. It presents a wide-ranging and detailed training program for the aspiring professional actor. Though widely used, teachers reported that *The Actor at Work* was too detailed and too advanced for many beginning students, and for students who wanted to enhance their appreciation of acting without necessarily embarking on a professional career. I decided, therefore, to write *The Actor in You* specifically for these students.

Teaching beginning acting is a demanding assignment that requires a crystal clear understanding of the acting process; to write *The Actor in You*, I had to identify the most crucial elements of the art, find a way to express them in simple language, and arrange them in a logical and effective sequence. This process was a valuable experience for me, and with the assistance of reviews written by classroom teachers who have used the book, the three subsequent editions have extended my own developing understanding of the art of acting in all its forms.

This fourth edition contains a substantial amount of new material requested by users, including entirely new chapters. Specifically, there is new material on the modern schools of thought about acting, new material on script analysis, and expanded material on movement. There is also improved presentation of former material, especially the crucial concept of action. I hope it is as useful for you in your work as it has been for me to write it.

PREFACE

This fourth edition has been revised according to suggestions from users of the previous editions. It offers sixteen easy steps that lead to an understanding and experience of the acting process. It is designed for students at the introductory level, whether they are beginning a training process as actors, or merely want to enhance their understanding and appreciation of the actor's art.

The sixteen steps are arranged in four parts. Part One uses examples drawn from everyday life to explain the basic principles of acting for stage or screen. Each concept is put to work in a simple improvisational or game-playing exercise. Part Two offers enjoyable exercises to prepare for creative group work in a relaxed and effective way. Part Three offers a step-by-step approach to basic text analysis. In this part, students will begin to prepare a simple, short, contemporary scene. Part Four outlines the actual process of rehearsing and performing the scene.

Throughout, examples will be used from four widely available plays: Arthur Miller's *Death of a Salesman*, Lorraine Hansberry's *A Raisin in the Sun*, Luis Valdez's *Zoot Suit*, and Tennessee Williams's *The Glass Menagerie*. I urge you to read each of these plays in order to better understand my examples. In addition, a scene from the television show *Cheers* is provided in Appendix A.

Teacher's Guide

You can download a free Teacher's Guide at www.robertbenedetti.com.

Acknowledgments

My thanks to the many students and colleagues who have contributed to my understanding of the acting process, either by their teaching or by their artistry. Thanks also to those who reviewed the manuscript for this edition: Matthew Andrews, Marist College; Johnna Maiorella, Adirondack Community College; Ray Miller, Appalachian State University; and Sara Nalley, Columbia College.

ABOUT THE AUTHOR

A distinguished teacher of acting and directing, and multiple Emmy and Peabody Award–winning film producer, Robert Benedetti received his Ph.D. from Northwestern University. He was an early member of Chicago's Second City Theatre, then taught acting for over forty years at schools such as the University of Wisconsin, Carnegie Mellon University, The National Theatre School of Canada, the University of California, Riverside, and the University of Nevada, Las Vegas. He was Chairman of Theatre at York University in Toronto, Head of the Acting Program at the Yale Drama School, and Dean of Theatre at The California Institute of the Arts.

Mr. Benedetti has directed at many regional theaters, including the Guthrie Theatre and the Melbourne Theatre Company, and at the Oregon, Colorado, and Great Lakes Shakespeare festivals.

As a film writer and producer, he won Emmys and a Peabody award for producing *Miss Evers' Boys* and *A Lesson before Dying* for HBO and has written and produced numerous other films.

Mr. Benedetti has written six books on acting and film production, including *The Actor at Work*, Tenth Edition; *ACTION! Acting for Film and Television*; and *From Concept to Screen*. In 2005, he received the Lifetime Career Achievement Award from the Association for Theatre in Higher Education. His first novel, *The Long Italian Goodbye*, was published in 2005. He can be reached at www.robertbenedetti.com.

The Actor in You

PART ONE

The Actor's Art

There are many reasons to study acting: Some of you may be considering a professional career; some of you may think the study of acting will help you present yourselves more effectively in everyday life; others may simply wish to better understand acting to enhance their enjoyment of plays, film, and TV shows.

Whatever your reason, you will hopefully discover that the study of acting can be a process of self-exploration that can expand your spiritual, psychological, and physical potentials. A psychologist who also teaches acting lists some of the ways in which the study of acting can contribute to personal growth:

> Finding our inner identity. Changing ourselves. Realizing and integrating our life experience. Seeing life freshly and with insight into others. Becoming aware of the powers of our mind. Risking and commitment. Learning how to concentrate our lives into the present, and the secrets of presence and charisma. Extending our sense of who we are, and achieving liberation from restricted concepts of what a person is.[1]

This last way, *achieving liberation*, may be especially important to you if you feel unduly limited in your behavior and emotional life by limits imposed by your personality, family, peer group, or cultural tradition.

One word of warning: Several of the exercises in this book require physical contact between students (as does the acting process itself) and this may be uncomfortable for you at first. If it is, share your concern privately with your teacher. Then, if you wish, you can—with your teacher's support—use your exploration of the acting process to begin overcoming physical shyness and to become more confident and comfortable in your physical identity.

In this, or perhaps other ways, the study of acting may help you to grow as a person; but even if the study of acting serves no immediate personal purpose, it

---

[1]Brian Bates, *The Way of the Actor* (Boston: Shambhala, 1987), p. 7.

1

can give you an enhanced understanding of real-life behavior, especially the way people act and react in pursuit of their needs and desires.

In all these ways, the study of acting, even if it does not lead to a professional career, is a meaningful journey of personal discovery and expansion. Through acting you can both explore your own thoughts and feelings, have experiences far beyond what your real life offers you, live in new worlds, and say and do things you would never be able to experience otherwise.

What a wonderful thing to do!

STEP

1 Understanding the Actor's Job and Tradition

In the most simple sense, an actor is anyone who performs a role in a play, TV show, or movie. These three different media, and the many different kinds of material performed in each, make different demands on actors. Few actors are equally good at all of them. A good TV sitcom actor, for instance, may not do well in a dramatic feature film. However, there are certain basic things that *all* good actors in any medium must do.

First, every good actor strives to create a performance that is *entertaining*. We often use this term to mean a light, diverting experience, but true entertainment can mean much more. The word *entertainment* comes from roots that literally mean "to enter" and "to hold," in the sense of something that enters us and becomes part of us, at least for a time; therefore, true entertainment provides a memorable experience which will stay with us after the performance is over and may even change us.

Long ago, the philosopher Aristotle wondered how a play that presents a painful spectacle, such as the tragedy *Oedipus Rex*, could nonetheless be entertaining. His answer was that we can enjoy watching a painful play because we appreciate both the skill of the performance and because we can learn something truthful from the experience. Therefore, the good actor strives to be not only entertaining, but also *skillful* and *truthful*. Consider first the matter of *skill*.

Though great actors have extraordinary physical, vocal, and spiritual skills, in a basic way actors do things we all do: they speak, move, and have thoughts, emotions, and personalities. What makes actors special is not so much *what* they do, but the special *way* in which they do it. You already have many of the skills you need to be an actor; what you need to learn are the actor's special ways of using those skills in a heightened and purified way. We often speak of the actor's physical and vocal skills as his or her *craft*, and it is interesting that the word *craft* comes from the German word for *power*. It is part of the ethical responsibility of the good actor to use this power for a meaningful and truthful purpose.

Though great skill is required, the actor's skill should never draw attention to itself in the sense of "showing off" or trying to get the audience's attention in inappropriate ways. What attracts us to great actors are the same things that make us watch star athletes: their effortless skill, their total concentration on the job at hand, and their tremendous sense of aliveness. We marvel at the "artlessness," the transparency of the actor who can make us forget that we are watching a performance and transport us completely into the world of the story. Actors who are able to work in this way become compelling; we sometimes say that we "can't take our eyes off" them.

Next we consider Aristotle's requirement that good drama must be *truthful*. The idea of "truth" in the theater and in films is relative to the style and content of the material: The naturalism of Stanislavski, the presentationalism of Meyerhold, the demonstrative Epic style of Brecht, the heightened physicality of Grotowski, and so on, all were the result of an effort to find and express theatrical truth, to create and present experiences that would relate to our lives in a meaningful way, perhaps even have the capacity to change us. Even material meant to be a pleasant "escape," like a TV sitcom, is more valuable if it offers some measure of truthfulness and insight. So we will say that a good actor strives to create a performance that is truthful—that is, relevant to the lives of the spectators—within the manner and content of the particular piece being performed.

Good actors also strive to be *believable*. They make us feel that we can recognize their characters as real human beings within the particular world of the story. Believability doesn't always mean "true to everyday life." Not all stories take place in everyday life; they may be set in an historical period, some other culture, or in a fantasy world. It is the world of the story that establishes what is "real"; the actor's performance has to be believable within that world. Every theater and film experience can have its own kind of reality and truth, and the good actor strives to serve each appropriately and skillfully.

Finally, it is not enough for an actor to be entertaining, skillful, truthful, and believable. A truly good performance must also *contribute to the particular story being told*. Every character in a story has been created by the writer to do a certain job within the world of that story. There are many things characters may be created to do: they may move the plot forward, provide an obstacle to some other character, provide information, represent some value or idea, provide "comic relief," and so on. Whatever the character was created to do, the actor must above all else create a performance that successfully fulfills that particular job. We will call this the *dramatic function* of the role. Fulfilling this dramatic function is the most important responsibility of a good actor.

To sum up, all good actors strive to fulfill the dramatic function of their role in an entertaining, skillful, truthful, and believable way. That's a lot to ask of the actor, and not even the best actors always achieve all these qualities in every performance. But these are the qualities that all good actors strive for in their work.

EXERCISE 1.1: WRITING A FILM OR TV REVIEW

Pick a performance you have seen recently in a film or TV show that made a strong impression on you. Write a review of it that examines the qualities discussed thus far. In what ways was the actor's performance *entertaining, skillful, truthful,* and *believable?* How did it serve the *dramatic function* of the character within the story? Did you feel the needs of the character? Were you compelled by what the character did to try to fulfill those needs? Did you feel yourself to be in his or her place?

The Tradition of the Actor

As you begin your study of acting, you should be aware of the long tradition to which the actor belongs. A sense of tradition can inform and enhance your work, and be a great source of energy and courage.

Our Western acting tradition began with religious festivals in ancient Greece when towns would send male choric groups to compete against one another in the recitation of poems as offerings to Dionysus, the god of wine, transformation, and the life force itself. Gradually, a chorus leader began to speak as an individual character, and many historians consider the chorus leader to be the prototype of the actor. Eventually two other actors were added, thus creating dialogue, and so plays as we know them were born. In 534 B.C., a contest for tragedy was established in Athens and was won by the first known actor, Thespis; the word *thespian* comes from his name. These early actors wore masks to indicate the characters they played, and each actor appeared in several parts.

Over the next thousand years, the foundations of our Western traditions shifted from Greece to Rome. The Roman actors no longer wore masks, and plays became more spectacular, as well as more violent and indecent. When the Roman church rose to power, it outlawed the theater, and around 400 A.D. actors were excommunicated. They remained outside the graces of the church—and polite society—for more than a thousand years thereafter.

Actors survived the Middle Ages mainly as traveling troubadours, telling stories in verse and song. These itinerant performers served the important function of carrying local dialects from one region to another, helping to create the national languages of Europe and England as we know them today.

The rebirth of the drama began in the 900s with brief playlets telling biblical stories performed by priests and choirboys in Latin as part of church services. Beginning in the 1200s, religious plays were expanded and moved outdoors; the actors were no longer priests or choirboys but members of nonreligious organizations such as trade guilds, like the rustics portrayed in Shakespeare's *A Midsummer Night's Dream.* Meanwhile, in the universities, plays were being written imitating classical Greek drama; these were produced in small private theaters for the aristocracy, and were often performed by the courtiers themselves.

The rebirth of the professional actor happened about this time, not in the church or university, but in the banquet hall and courtyard. The nobility began to accompany dinners and other social events with comedic skits acted out by skilled performers. To supply these performances, troupes of actors began to travel from household to household, like the players in Shakespeare's *Hamlet*, performing comical interludes based on folktales. Meanwhile, in Italy, the Commedia dell'Arte featured a traditional cast of characters and improvised dialogue. All these kinds of traveling players performed for nobility but also sometimes in market squares and at public festivals, eking out a living from their craft.

Elizabethan plays developed in the late 1500s when a new group of playwrights merged the interludes performed by wandering actors with the classically inspired plays of the universities. To perform these plays, companies of professional actors were formed under the sponsorship of noble persons, and the business of public theater as we know it was born. The actors in these companies received regular salaries, and the leading actors were shareholders who received a portion of the box office income, much like today's movie stars who have profit–participation deals.

Acting continued to develop as a profession throughout the 1600s with the emergence of companies run by strong actor/managers. Up to this time, all female parts had been played by young boys (there were even all-boy companies), but in the 1660s actresses began to appear regularly on the English stage. For many years these actresses were widely regarded (with some justification) as women of loose morals. In fact, up to this time both male and female actors were still denied burial in consecrated ground.

During the 1700s, actors became increasingly important and respected. Audiences were attracted to star performers rather than to particular plays. In the 1740s, David Garrick brought greater realism to English acting, although the dominant style of acting for the next 150 years would seem artificial by today's standards.

It was not until the turn of the twentieth century, with the work of Constantin Stanislavski (1863–1938) and his Moscow Art Theatre, that the truly modern actor was born, an actor devoted to searching for the truth of human behavior through systematic discipline and to making the world a better place through the ideas and experiences the actor could bring to the audience. Stanislavski's approach soon established itself as the dominant technique from his time to the present day. In its earliest form, Stanislavski's work stressed psychological and emotional techniques that encouraged the actor to work "from the inside out." Later, however, he switched to a more physical approach called "the Method of Physical Actions" (more on this in Step 3).

At the same time, a contemporary of Stanislavski, Vsevolod Meyerhold, (1874–1940), developed another kind of acting focused not on the psychology of behavior but on the structure of the body, which Meyerhold called *biomechanics*. Borrowing from Asian theater and reviving the storytelling spirit of the itinerant performer, Meyerhold's approach was *presentational* and overtly theatrical. His approach became an alternative tradition that paralleled Stanislavski's and inspired various avant-garde experiments throughout the twentieth century.

A few years later, a German playwright and director, Bertolt Brecht (1898–1956), borrowed elements of both Stanislavski's and Meyerhold's methods to create an overtly political actor who could *demonstrate* the character's behavior while still expressing a judgment on it. The Brechtian tradition remains important today, especially in political theaters such as the San Francisco Mime Troupe.

In the social ferment of the 1960s and 1970s many avant-garde theaters, such as The Living Theatre, The Open Theatre, and The Polish Laboratory Theatre, developed individual approaches to acting, borrowing elements from Stanislavski, Meyerhold, and Brecht. These alternative acting techniques have several things in common. First and most notably, like Meyerhold's, they are all primarily physical in their approach. They stress body and vocal work in the training of actors, and extraordinary uses of the body and voice in performance. Second, they are all aimed at creating theater experiences that produce powerful spiritual changes in the audience, experiences communicated primarily through physical rather than intellectual means. (In this, they mirror the rise of alternative methods of psychotherapy during the twentieth century, when Reichian and other body-based therapies arose as alternatives to Freudian talking therapy.)

Meyerhold's biomechanics, for example, used physical training to forge the connection between mind and body, to "teach the body to think." It began with simple activities like running and jumping, then progressed to leaps and rolls, movement with objects, up and down ramps and stairs, partner lifts, and acrobatics, culminating in highly stylized movement pieces choreographed by Meyerhold himself. Eventually, Meyerhold's actor achieved a state of total mind–body integration.

The tradition springing from Meyerhold's approach developed throughout the mid-twentieth century. The ideas of French actor/director Antonin Artaud (1896–1948) were especially influential even though he never developed a specific body of technique. His central concepts were that the actor sacrifices him- or herself in the act of performing; that the poetry of theater is primarily movement and sound rather than words; that the actor's movement and sound has its own meanings and penetrates the spectator directly; and that the resulting experience can move the spectators to heightened spiritual experience that forces them to confront their true nature.

The Polish director Jerzy Grotowski (1933–1999) used Artaud's ideas to develop a training program and body of technique based on the idea of the "Holy" actor, meaning an actor who surrendered the self totally in the act of performing. This sacrifice was achieved by rigorous physical and vocal training (called "plastique" exercises) so extreme that they broke down all obstacles between impulse and expression and therefore made deception or censorship impossible. The authentic soul of the actor in performance became visible, and experiencing such a performance could encourage the audience to begin to live in a similar way.

Other theater makers such as Joseph Chaikin, Jacques Lecoq, Ariane Mnouchkine, Tadashi Suzuki, and many others, have expanded on these ideas and developed approaches of their own. The evolution of the actor has continued to the present day as serious training programs have assimilated all these and many other influences, opening themselves as well to the wealth of non-Western world theater. This has produced a rich broth of philosophies and techniques in which you can find a place for your own unique energies. It is a wonderful time to become an actor!

Getting into the Tradition

An important part of your study of acting will be to immerse yourself in the living tradition of the theater, past and present.

You can study the past by reading books on theater history and taking classes in it. You can also keep up with current theater events by reading journals like *American Theatre Magazine*, including its online version at www.tcg.org, and other interesting online sites like *Playbill* at www.playbill.com. Newspaper articles and reviews like those in *The New York Times* (also available online) and theater columns in magazines can also help keep you up to date.

Most important, of course, try to see as much live theater as you can. Although there is wonderful acting to be seen in movies and television, the live stage experience is special. Being part of the living community that is a theater audience, and watching the live performer, has an immediacy that film performance cannot duplicate: as Orson Welles once said, "It is no accident that movies come in cans." So don't miss opportunities to attend live performances every chance you get. Keeping a theater journal and writing reviews can help you learn from your theater-going experiences.

EXERCISE 1.2: WRITING A STAGE REVIEW

As soon as possible, see a live performance and write a review of the work of one of the actors. Ask the same questions as you did in your film review: how was the actor's performance *entertaining, skillful, truthful,* and *believable?* How did it serve the *dramatic function* of the character? Pay special attention to the qualities of the live experience; how was it different from a film experience? How was the actor's performance changed by being in front of a live audience?

Summary of Step 1

All good actors, whether on stage or screen, strive to create characters who fulfill the dramatic function for which they were created, and to do so in an entertaining, skillful, truthful, and believable way.

The long tradition of the actor has its earliest spiritual roots in the celebration of Dionysus, god of transformational life force. In the twentieth century, Stanislavski, Meyerhold, Brecht, Artaud, and others expanded the role of the actor, and this evolution has continued to the present day. An important part of your study of acting will be to immerse yourself in this living tradition of the theater, past and present.

STEP

2 Discovering Action

Consider the word *actor*. At its root, it means someone who "acts," who *does* something. Think for a moment: why do you do things in everyday life?

Usually, you do things in order to get something you *need*. Sometimes what you need is related to physical survival: food, money, or shelter. Sometimes your need is emotional: to be loved, to find peace or beauty. Whatever your need, if it is urgent enough, you *do* something about it. You *act* in order to achieve some objective that you hope will satisfy your need.

Characters in plays, TV shows, and movies are shown in situations when something important is happening. In such dramatic situations, whether funny or sad, the needs of the characters are heightened; they are compelled to try to satisfy those needs by doing often extraordinary things. This is what makes the story interesting to us; we can feel ourselves in the place of the characters because we also try to do things to fulfill our needs every day, though not usually in such extraordinary ways or circumstances. We feel *suspense* as we wait to see whether the characters will get what they need or not. Will Oedipus find the killer of Laius? Will Romeo and Juliet get together? Will Spiderman save the world?

This basic definition of acting will be at the heart of everything in this book: *immediate and urgent needs cause actions in the pursuit of objectives within given circumstances.* This is a complex idea; read it aloud several times and become aware of each of the elements it contains: needs, actions, objectives, and circumstances. We will explore each of these elements in later steps.

This view of acting as "doing," rather than "showing" or "telling about," is the single most important and profound concept in the contemporary view of the actor's art. It is summed up by the term *action*, and you cannot understand the modern idea of acting without understanding the idea of action.

We can go all the way back to 350 B.C. and Aristotle's *Poetics*, the very first writing about Western drama, to begin understanding this idea of action. The main difference between drama and other kinds of writing, Aristotle said, is that the drama shows us a thing happening *as if before our eyes* and *for the first time*. Other kinds of writing can tell us a story, and may even contain dramatic elements, but a play presents the story as something happening right now, right here. A play is not "about" something; it *is* the event itself.

Just so, the good actor's performance is not "about" the character, it "is" the character living before our eyes as if for the first time. That is why we say that acting is *doing*, not showing or telling. Like the play itself, the actor has to be here and now, doing the thing itself as if for the first time, *in action*.

Action is expressed in many ways: physical, vocal, intellectual, emotional, and spiritual. When an actor is truly in action, all these aspects of the performance combine into one unified state and become interconnected: an adjustment in the body can generate a change of emotion, a change in the voice can generate new thoughts and emotions, a new emotional experience can generate physical and vocal changes, and so on. Acting can be approached in all of these ways, and the best actor training programs simultaneously address them all.

This is why so many different acting techniques can all produce good results, though one or another may be more effective for any individual actor. Whether they approach acting primarily through the body, the voice, the mind, the emotions, or the spirit, all contemporary acting techniques are aimed at creating a dynamic actor who does things in a total, authentic, and dramatically effective way, rather than an actor who merely shows off, or shows us the image or idea of the character instead of the character in action.

Stanislavski's View of Action

Constantin Stanislavski was one of the first to explore the idea of action in a systematic way. He was dissatisfied with the overblown acting style of his time; too often, he felt, the actor's display of emotion and technique became an end in itself and overshadowed the meaning of the play. Stanislavski set out to create a new system of acting aimed at economy, greater psychological truthfulness, and above all respect for the ideas of the play.

He based his system on the idea that everything an actor does in a performance has to be *justified* by the character's internal need. As Stanislavski said:

> There are no physical actions divorced from some desire, some effort in some direction, some objective. . . . Everything that happens on the stage has a definite purpose.[1]

According to this principle, everything the actor does as the character should grow directly out of the needs of the character, so that the "inner" world of the character and the "outer" world of the performance are unified. This is what he called a "truthful" performance (more on this in Step 3).

---

[1]Constantin Stanislavski, *An Actor's Handbook*, trans. and ed. Elizabeth Reynolds Hapgood (New York: Theatre Arts Books, 1936), p. 8. Copyright © 1936, 1961, 1963 by Elizabeth Reynolds Hapgood.

This book is based on a particular interpretation of Stanislavski's idea. The central concept is that at each moment of the performance, your character wants something (your *need*) which makes you do something (your *action*) in an effort to achieve a desired goal (your *objective*). Some schools of acting use the terms *intention* or *task* instead of *objective*, but they all mean the same thing.

To put it even more simply, *need causes an action directed toward an objective*. We will explore each element of this idea in later steps, but for now, reread it aloud several times and feel the *flow* of energy from need to action toward objective.

The power of this approach is that your attention as an actor, in rehearsal and performance, is focused on the character's objective; this focus brings you many benefits, such as concentration, relaxation, economy, spontaneity, and reduction in self-awareness (all of which you will explore in later Steps). Best of all, however, this focus helps to put you *into* your character in an active way: you *want* what the character wants in his or her circumstances, and you *do* what the character does to try to get it. This gives you a living experience of the character and leads to what Stanislavski called *transformation* as you become a new version of yourself.

Here is a simple exercise to help you begin to experience focus of attention on an objective.

EXERCISE 2.1: A SIMPLE TASK

Select a simple physical activity which requires great concentration, such as building a house of cards, counting the floorboards or tiles on the floor, or balancing a stick on your nose. Perform this task in front of your class; can you allow yourself to become so absorbed in it that you "forget" that you are in front of an audience?

Although the aim of Stanislavski's approach is the creation of a "truthful" performance—meaning that the actor is really doing what the character does and thereby has transformed him- or herself into a living embodiment of the character—Stanislavski was not satisfied unless the performance also correctly served the *needs of the play*. He stressed that the actor cannot use his or her transformational skills for their own sake, nor create emotion for its own sake, but rather strives to discover how every moment of the performance contributes to *the reason why the play was written*. This is what we meant when we spoke of *dramatic function* in Step 1.

For example, in Arthur Miller's *Death of a Salesman*, the actors playing Willy Loman's neighbor, Charley, and the ghost of Willy's brother, Ben, must understand that their characters were created to present alternative ways of living between which Willy must choose. Unlike Willy, Charley accepts who he is and lives happily; Ben, in contrast, represents the American Dream, making a fortune by daring and struggle. If Willy could learn to live like Charley instead of Ben, it would save Willy's life. The actors playing the roles of Charley and Ben create their performances with this in mind. (Arthur Miller even provides a scene in which Willy tries to talk to each of these characters at the same time, and becomes hopelessly trapped between them.)

This sense of the dramatic function of a character is often discovered gradually in the early stages of rehearsal. It gives the actor a goal that inspires and guides the exploration of the rehearsal process, and provides a sense of priority in judging the value and correctness of discoveries made in rehearsal. A good actor avoids doing anything that does not serve the dramatic purpose of the character, and thereby achieves *economy*, which is one of the aspects of beauty and truthfulness.

Making Action Stageworthy

We began by saying that you "act" in everyday life when you do things in order to get what you want or need. The art of acting is based on this everyday process, but actions and their expression must be heightened and purified for artistic purposes. In the following steps you will learn specific techniques to achieve this, but for now, let's consider the principles involved in making actions stageworthy.

When you are trying to do something really important in real life, it commands your whole attention, and all your energy and awareness flow through your action toward your objective. In acting, we say that a person fully committed to an important objective is *in action*. You have seen people with this kind of total commitment to an action: an athlete executing a difficult play, people arguing a deeply felt issue, a student studying for a big test, lovers wooing. All these people are in action because *they have an objective that is so personally significant that they are totally focused on what they are doing*. The more important the objective, the stronger the action and complete the focus. In acting, we call this *raising the stakes*.

There are various ways of raising the stakes. A good writer will often provide a scene with circumstances that raise the stakes by giving the outcome special significance, by creating some obstacle to the action, or by creating a deadline that encourages a sense of urgency. Actors learn to recognize these conditions and make the most of them in playing the scene.

The actor can also raise the stakes for him- or herself by finding in the character's situation some need or objective that has true personal significance. Sometimes, this requires substituting for the character's need some analogous need or objective that touches the actor personally. This will often happen automatically in rehearsal as you begin to experience the world and actions of the character and are reminded of similar needs, beliefs, and circumstances from your own life. These can become the bedrock on which you will build the character, and no amount of "acting" can substitute for the real personal energy that results.

EXERCISE 2.2: RAISING THE STAKES

Think about a time when something happened to you that made you try to do something really important, when you were fully in action and the stakes were high. Relive this incident in your imagination, then try to recreate it as a scene for your class; enlist the participation of others in the class if necessary. Remember that your aim is to recreate the experience itself; avoid "showing" or "telling" about it.

There are several benefits to the actor in raising the stakes by finding needs, objectives, and circumstances that are important to him or her in a personal way. First, people reveal a great deal about themselves when they are fully committed to an important action, perhaps more than at any other time. As we say, "actions speak louder than words." When people are fully in action, they are pouring all their energy and awareness into what they are doing, and have none left over for deception or self-consciousness. As a result, we judge them as *authentic* and *believable*. We also find people who are fully in action *compelling* to watch; they seem so alive and energized that they command our full attention.

To sum up: being in action makes you more *alive, authentic, believable,* and *compelling.* In addition, as we will see in a later step, being in action can also help the actor to conquer those great enemies, self-consciousness and stage fright.

These are all powerful reasons why being in action, being fully focused on a personally significant objective, is the best condition for you as an actor. This will be the goal of each of the steps you will take in this book.

Using Action in a Scene

Now it is time to put your sense of action to work within the context of a dramatic scene. As a first step, you will begin with a simple improvisation. Keep this exercise simple; it doesn't need to be long, complicated, witty, or dramatic. Just let it be as real and natural as possible. Go with whatever comes up and see where it leads.

EXERCISE 2.3: A SIMPLE ACTION SCENE

With a partner, select a simple situation in which one of you wants to do something (like "to leave the room") while the other has a contradictory objective (like "to make him or her stay"). Think of a circumstance that raises the stakes: a deadline or consequence that creates urgency.

1. Without premeditation, and using a minimum of words, both attempt to achieve their objectives in the most simple, direct terms.
2. Repeat the exercise, but this time each of you privately invents a powerful *need* for doing what you are doing. For example, one of you might imagine that if the other gets out, he or she will hurt someone you love; the other might imagine that he or she needs to get out to save a loved one. You needn't share what your needs are, nor do you need to agree on your needs.
3. Repeat the exercise again, this time imagining that you are both in a place where you cannot make much noise or movement, such as a public library or a funeral.

Discuss the experience of this exercise:

1. Did you maintain your awareness of your objective throughout?
2. Did you adjust what you did in reaction to what your partner did?
3. What was the effect of adding strong needs?
4. What was the effect of changing the circumstance?
5. Did you notice how drama, emotion, and even a sense of character arose naturally from the action of the exercise?

These questions are fundamental to the acting process, and all will be explored in greater detail in the remainder of this book.

Summary of Step 2

Drama shows us a thing happening *as if before our eyes* and *for the first time*. Just so, the good actor's performance is not "about" the character, it "is" the character living before our eyes as if for the first time. That is why we say that acting is *doing*, not showing or telling. Stanislavski based his system on the idea that everything an actor does in a performance has to be *justified* by connecting it to an internal need in the character. The main idea is that *need causes an action directed toward an objective*. In everyday life, people are in action when *they have an objective that is so personally significant that they are totally focused on what they are doing*; in acting, we call this *raising the stakes*. Being in action in this way makes you more *alive, authentic, believable*, and *compelling*. A good writer will often provide circumstances that raise the stakes. The actor can also raise the stakes for him- or herself by finding in the character's situation some need or objective that has true personal significance.

STEP

3   Experiencing Internal and External Action

Action is not just external activity. A cat watching a mouse hole is not moving at all, yet we recognize the drama, the sense of "significant doing," in it. This is because action is felt even before it has shown itself in external activity; it lives even in the *potential* for doing. At such moments, the action is literally living inside us, waiting to erupt into the outside world. You can see, then, that we experience both *internal* and *external* action.

Stanislavski called internal action *spiritual*, and external action *physical:*

> The creation of the physical life is half the work on a role because, like us, a role has two natures, physical and spiritual . . . a role on the stage, more than action in real life, must bring together the two lives—of external and internal action—in mutual effort to achieve a given purpose.[1]

When we have connected an external action with the internal action that motivates it, Stanislavski would say that we have *justified* the action. For Stanislavski it was this justification, this complete integration of internal and external action, that produced a truthful stage performance. Accordingly, his acting system was designed to bring about this integration. In the beginning, he used psychological techniques that were designed to work from the internal to the external (from the inside out). Later in the development of his method, he began to work from the external toward the internal (from the outside in). As he said, our inner condition is affected by our outer action just as much as our outer action is caused by our inner condition:

> The spirit cannot but respond to the actions of the body, provided of course that these are genuine, have a purpose . . . [In this way] a part acquires inner content [through the development of outer actions.][2]

---

[1]Constantin Stanislavski, *Building a Character*, trans. Elizabeth Reynolds Hapgood (New York: Theatre Arts Books, 1949), pp. 218–36.

[2]Constantin Stanislavski, *Creating a Role*, trans. Elizabeth Reynolds Hapgood (New York: Theatre Arts Books, 1961), p. 62.

Many have wondered whether the actor should work from the inside out or from the outside in. Throughout the modern period, various techniques have been developed that fall on one side or the other of this question. In general, during the first half of the twentieth century the British acting tradition stressed the importance of externals in the acting process, working "from the outside in," whereas the American tradition stressed the importance of internals, working "from the inside out," most notably in the work of Lee Strasberg, founder of the Actors Studio, who placed great emphasis on emotional and sensory memory.

Since the 1950s, however, most training programs on both sides of the Atlantic have tried to integrate these approaches. The aim is now for a total integration of internals and externals, for both are essential, as Stanislavski pointed out:

> External action acquires inner meaning and warmth from inner action, while [inner action] finds its expression only in physical terms.[3]

If your action consists only of external movement and speech unconnected to an inner energy, it will seem hollow and lifeless. If your action lives only as inner intensity, without skillful outer expression, it will seem vague and self-indulgent. The most useful approach, then, is to avoid thinking of "inner" and "outer" action as being in any way separate. *Imagine instead a single flow of action that has both an inner phase and an outer phase.*

Here is how this flow works: something happens to which you respond, causing your aroused inner energy to flow outward and to become external action. When this happens naturally, you experience the inner and outer aspects of the flow as a single action. Here is an exercise to help you experience that flow.

EXERCISE 3.1: IMPULSE CIRCLE

1. With your entire group, sit in a large circle, in chairs or on the floor, about eighteen inches apart. Make the circle perfectly round. All group members put their left hands out palm up, then rest their right hands lightly on top of the left hands of those to their right.

   The leader will now start a small, clean slap with his or her right hand. The slap is passed on from person to person around the circle. Once the slap is moving well, try the following experiments:

   a. Focus your awareness on the slap as it moves around the circle. Begin to experience it as having a life of its own. Notice how it changes.

---

[3]Constantin Stanislavski, *An Actor's Handbook*, trans. and ed. Elizabeth Reynolds Hapgood (New York: Theatre Arts Books, 1936), p. 9. Copyright © 1936, 1961, 1963, by Elizabeth Reynolds Hapgood.

b. Now allow the slap to move as quickly as it can. See what happens when you "get out of its way." Do not force it to go faster; simply relax and react to it as instantaneously as possible.

c. Now let it slow down. See how slowly it can go without dying. Keep the external slap sharp and quick, but slow down the inner impulse as it travels within each of you. Become aware of how the slap flows through both internal and external phases.

2. Drop your hands, and discuss the many ways in which this exercise is like a scene in a performance. Consider these questions:

a. What made it possible for the slap to flow around the group? How is this similar to the way a scene should flow in a performance?

b. As you experienced the slap as having a life of its own, how did the nature of the flow change? Did your own experience of it change?

c. Did allowing it to be the focus of your awareness reduce your self-consciousness?

d. How much of the time was it "invisible" as a purely internal action? When it was slow, were there times when it was completely internal? Were such moments any less dramatic?

e. What was different about the experience when it was moving slowly? What did you need to do to support its life, even while it was passing through the others in the circle?

f. What are some of the ways in which a scene can "die"? What are some of the ways in which we can fail to "pass it on"? How do actors make similar mistakes in performance?

3. Repeat the exercise using a sound such as "Ho" instead of a slap.

(Repeat this exercise on subsequent days for a good group warm-up.)

In this exercise you experienced how energy flows between people, taking both external and internal forms. It is external when someone is saying or doing something, but much of the time it is internal as every participant receives the energy from others, reacts to it, and then passes it on through responsive action.

In the same way, a scene in a play or screenplay depends on energy flowing from character to character as each one reacts and acts to the other. This flow of action and reaction is a give-and-take, as it moves the scene forward and eventually creates the unfolding of the entire story. Therefore we often say that *acting is reacting*.

Interactions

In the impulse circle exercise (3.1), the slap or sound traveled through the group, each person receiving and in turn passing on the energy so that it could take on a life of its own. You learned from this exercise that it is the flow of action and reaction between the characters that moves a scene. It follows, then, that you and your partners must be good at receiving and sending energy, whatever form it may take—words, gestures, glances, silences, and so on.

When energy is passed from one person to another, we call it an *interaction*. Each interaction is a connection in the flow of action and reaction that moves the scene and the entire story. Actors work hard to build each interaction in a scene, to make each of them real, and to make sure each moves toward the ultimate destination of the scene, and the story as a whole.

Remember also how the slap took on a life of its own and began to flow smoothly. When energy is flowing smoothly, the interactions from actor to actor become a continuous process of receiving and sending, leading and following, in which all the actors are both senders and receivers, leaders and followers simultaneously. The following exercises will give you the experience of this simultaneous leading and following.

EXERCISE 3.2: LEADING AND FOLLOWING

1. *Blind leading.* You and your partner lightly interlace fingertips up to the first joint. Your partner closes his or her eyes, and you silently lead him or her around the room. As you gain confidence and control, begin to move faster and extend the range of your travels. Soon you can run! If your situation permits, you can even take a trip to some distant destination. Reverse roles and repeat for the trip back.
2. *Sound leading.* Begin as above, but when you are well under way, break physical contact and begin to lead your partner by repeating a single word which your partner follows by sound alone. Again, extend your range and speed. Run! *Caution: Be prepared to grab your partner to prevent a collision!*

Review the experience of this exercise. As a follower, did you trust your partner enough to truly commit your weight to your movement? As leader, did you receive your partner's energy and respond to his or her momentum?

Let's continue with another exercise to explore simultaneous leading and following.

EXERCISE 3.3: MIRRORS

1. You and a partner decide who is "A" and who is "B." Stand facing each other. Person A makes slow "underwater" movements that B can mirror completely. Try to keep the partnership moving in unison. The movements flow in a continually changing stream; avoid repeated patterns. Bigger, more continuous movements are easier to follow.
2. At a signal, the roles are instantly reversed *without a break in the action*. B is now the leader; A is the follower. Continue moving from the deep centers of your bodies; feel yourselves beginning to share a common center through your shared movement; from it comes a common breathing and a common sound which arises naturally from your movement.
3. The roles are reversed a few more times; each time the leadership role changes, but the movement and sound continue without interruption.
4. Finally, there is no leader. Neither A nor B leads, but you continue to move and sound together.

Watch other partnerships doing this exercise: Do you see how intense and connected to each other they seem? Our listening and seeing of each other in performance should always have this kind of intensity; you will be leading and following each other during a scene just as much as you did in these exercises. Here's another exercise exploring this through sound (see Figure 3.1).

EXERCISE 3.4: COOKIE SEARCH

1. Everyone in the group chooses a partner. Then the entire group stands together in a clump at the center of the room with eyes closed. Then all spin around a few times until no one knows which way they are facing.
2. Without opening your eyes, move slowly in whatever direction you are facing until you reach a wall or other obstacle. Avoid touching anyone else; feel your way with all of your nonvisual senses.
3. When you have gone as far as you can (and still have not opened your eyes), begin to search for your partner using only the word *cookie*.
4. When you find each other, open your eyes and wait in silence for all to finish. Enjoy watching the others search. Feel the drama of the exercise.

FIGURE 3.1   A Cookie Search.

In this exercise you were not led but had to find your own way toward the sounds of your partner. Did you feel lonely while searching for your partner and relieved when you found him or her? Don't be the kind of actor who makes partners feel lonely during performance!

Summary of Step 3

Action has both an *internal* and *external* form. If action consists only of external activity unconnected to an inner energy, it will seem hollow and lifeless; if it is only an inner intensity, without skillful outer expression, it will seem vague and self-indulgent. Stanislavski believed it was the complete integration of internal and external action, which he called *justification*, that produced a truthful stage performance. The most useful approach, then, is to think of *a single flow of action which has both an inner phase and an outer phase.*

A scene lives because of the energy flowing from character to character as they *interact* through the flow of action and reaction, which moves the scene forward and eventually creates the unfolding of the entire story. This is why we often say that *acting is reacting*. When energy is flowing smoothly, the interactions from actor to actor become a continuous process of receiving and sending.

STEP

4 Understanding Emotion and Character

We've said that the process of acting is basically the pursuit of an objective in order to satisfy a need. Notice that this definition of acting does not mention *emotion*. People commonly think that the actor's job is to portray strong emotions, and although emotion can be an important part of a performance, a good actor does not approach the work in this way. He or she knows that genuine and specific emotion is achieved—on stage as in life—only as the *result* of trying to do something important. Trying to shortcut this process to create an emotion for its own sake is mere trickery lacking in truth for both actor and audience.

Likewise, in the acting process, actors too often think that they must *feel* something before they *do* anything. You sometimes hear them say, "I don't feel it yet." Of course you want to find the emotional state of your character so that your actions will have the proper quality and tone, but finding the right emotion is a *process* that takes some time. The emotion is the *result* of the process, not its starting point.

You begin work not with the emotion but with the material you get from the script—the words your character says and the actions they convey—and as you experience the action you discover the emotional life that it evokes. In other words, you *do* things in order to fulfill a need, and emotion naturally results from that doing.

This is how emotion works in real life; your emotions spring from your efforts to get what you want. Think of something you want desperately: if you get it, you are happy; if you don't, you are sad. If you don't get what you want and it is not your fault, you feel angry. When you don't get what you want and you don't know why, you feel afraid. In all these cases, you acted on your need first, and emotion followed; so it should be in performance. Remember: *action produces emotion, not the other way around.*

Even if a script gives you an indication of your character's emotional condition in a scene, you will not play that emotion; rather you will find it by experiencing the character's action while pursuing his or her objective in a way that results in the correct emotion. Trying to generate the emotion first is an unreliable and exhausting method that denies the way in which emotion functions in real life.

Character and the Magic If

In the same way that emotion arises from action, character emerges from action as well. This is how it happens in real life too, where we call character "personality." Think about how your own personality has developed over the years and how often you "create a character" in real life.

You play a role every time you enter a social situation. In various circumstances and relationships, you pursue your needs by behaving in certain ways, doing and saying certain things in certain ways to other people, and reacting to the things they do and say to you. It is this interaction with your world, this give-and-take of acting and reacting, that shapes and expresses your character in everyday life. It is an ongoing process: as your circumstances, needs, and relationships change, they cause changes in you as a person.

In fact, you play several roles every day—student, son or daughter, friend, employee—each with its own appropriate behavior, speech, thought, and feelings; your own little cast of characters!

This fact was noticed many years ago by the psychologist William James, who said that our personalities are actually composed of many social roles. He called these roles our various *me's*. Behind the me's, of course, there is one consciousness, which he called our *I*. But our I is not rigid and is expressed through all of our me's, even though some of them may be quite different from one another.

We may even experience situations in which two or more of our me's come into conflict with one another. If you are busy being "buddy" with your friends or "lover" with that special other, the arrival of a boss or parents may cause an uncomfortable conflict between your role as buddy or lover and your role as employee or child. Such situations are inherently dramatic and often occur in plays, as when Hamlet is torn between the roles of son, lover, friend, and avenger.

EXERCISE 4.1: ROLE-PLAYING IN LIFE

Think about your own experience over the past few days. What roles did you play? How did your situation influence your behavior and feelings? Were there times when you had to switch roles rapidly or when your roles came into conflict?

As you think about how you play various roles in your life, you will also notice that your sense of "I" tends to flow into whichever "me" you are being at the moment. Some of your me's may be more—or less—comfortable than others, but they are all versions of yourself. If you are in a circumstance that forces you to behave in a certain way, and you allow yourself to remain in that situation for a time, you start to become the kind of person appropriate to that situation; you develop a new me, and this in turn influences your I.

Just so, when you perform as an actor on stage or screen, you will learn to let your I flow into the new me of each role you play, even when that me is quite different from your everyday self. The qualities of each new me have been determined by the writer, who has also created a new set of circumstances, a new world, in which the new me lives. One of your most important skills as an actor will be *to allow your I to flow fully and freely into the new me of the role and its world.* You do this not to "be yourself" but to develop a new version of yourself, perhaps quite different from your everyday self, that is nevertheless "natural" to you, truthful to the character and the character's world as created by the writer, and appropriate to the artistic purpose for which the role was created.

Stanislavski described this process as the *Magic If.* He urged the actor to ask, "*If* I were in the situation of the character, and *if* I wanted what the character wants, what would I do?" This approach can create interesting and useful improvisations, but it may encourage actors to get used to inventing their own actions, which may not always be consistent with the specific demands of a given play. Although it is necessary for the actor to experience the character's needs, objectives, and actions as if they were his or her own, the actor does not have the freedom to alter the actions (the sayings and doings) specified by the script. Rather, he or she must *rediscover* the living process that lies beneath the dialogue and arrive at the result determined by the author.

We will therefore slightly modify Stanislavski's idea: *if* you allow yourself to live in the world of the character, and *if* you allow yourself to need what the character needs, and *if you allow yourself to do the things the character does* to try to satisfy those needs, you naturally, "magically," start to modify your thought, feelings, behavior, and even your body and voice toward that new version of yourself that will be your special way of playing the role. This is the true *transformation.*

This ability to become a fictitious character, to completely believe in the Magic If and enter a make-believe world and character, is something we all had naturally as children. It is this childlike ability for make-believe that we need to rediscover as actors, however much we empower it through our adult sense of purpose and technique.

EXERCISE 4.2: CHARACTER IN LIFE

For the next few days, observe your own behavior toward those around you. Notice the way you present yourself differently in various circumstances.

1. Notice changes in your physical behavior.
2. Notice changes in your voice, manner of speaking, and choice of words.
3. Notice your choice of clothing and the "props" you use.
4. Notice changes in the way you think and feel.
5. Most of all, notice how you naturally tend to "become" each of the roles you are playing.

Consider keeping an actor's journal in which you record such experiences and observations as they occur. Such a journal can help to clarify your thinking and give form to your ongoing development.

The Actor in You

You now understand that when an actor creates a character, the process is similar to what you do every day in real life. In this sense, you are already an actor, and you already have many of the skills you will need to perform on stage or screen. A sociologist noticed this fifty years ago when he said:

> It does take deep skill, long training, and psychological capacity to become a good stage actor. But . . . almost anyone can quickly learn a script well enough to give a charitable audience some sense of realness. . . . Scripts even in the hands of unpracticed players can come to life because life itself is a dramatically enacted thing. . . . In short, we all act better than we know how.[1]

Even though you already "act better than [you] know how," performing for the stage or camera requires that these everyday abilities be heightened, purified, and brought within the control of a purposeful discipline. As one acting teacher who is also a psychologist puts it,

> Almost everything that actors do can be identified with things we do in less dramatic form in everyday life. But in order to express the concentrated truths which are the life-stuff of drama, and to project convincing performances before large audiences, and the piercing eye of the film and television camera, the actor must develop depths of self-knowledge and powers of expression far beyond those with which most of us are familiar.[2]

This book will help you begin to develop your everyday acting skills into the greater power of artistic technique. Your job is to recognize, focus, and strengthen the natural actor you already are. Only you can do this, but the ideas and exercises in this book provide insights and experiences to help you fulfill your natural talents.

Summary of Step 4

As in everyday life, *action produces emotion and character, not the other way around.* This principle is fundamental to our approach to the acting process and explains how character is created.

According to William James, our personalities are composed of many social roles he called our *me's;* behind the me's there is one consciousness, our *I.* As an actor you will learn to let your I flow into the new me of each role so that it becomes "natural" to you, truthful to the character, and appropriate to the artistic purpose for which the role was created. Stanislavski called this process the

[1]Erving Goffman, T*he Presentation of Self in Everyday Life* (New York: Doubleday, 1959), pp. 71–74. Copyright © by Erving Goffman.

[2]Brian Bates, *The Way of the Actor* (Boston: Shambhala, 1987), p. 7.

Magic If. *If* you live in the world of the character, and *if* you need what the character needs, and *if* you do the things the character does to satisfy those needs, you naturally start to modify your thought, feelings, behavior, and even your body and voice; a new me begins to form—that new version of yourself which will be your special way of playing the role.

What an actor does, then, is similar to what you do every day in real life. In this sense, you are already an actor, and you already have many of the skills you will need to perform. It is the development of these everyday acting skills into the greater power of artistic technique that is the aim of your study.

Summary of Part One

You now understand the basic concepts involved in acting. We can summarize what we have learned so far.

1. The actor's job is to fulfill the dramatic purpose of the role in a believable, skillful, and truthful way.
2. Acting is being driven by an urgent and immediate *need* to commit an *action* to achieve an *objective* that will fulfill that need. All external actions on stage need to be *justified* by the inner process of need that causes the external action.
3. Action naturally produces emotion and character, not the other way around. You start with the *doing* and evolve toward the inner life that justifies it.
4. The Magic If allows your "I" to flow naturally into the new "me" of the created character. *If* you live in the world of the character and *if* you need what the character needs and *if* you do the things the character does to try to satisfy those needs, you naturally start to experience the life of the character and to modify your behavior and thought. This is the same process of give-and-take that develops your personality in real life.

Understanding these basic principles, you are ready now to prepare yourself to begin work as an actor.

PART TWO

Preparing Yourself to Act

You already understand that to be believable, all aspects of an actor's portrayal must work together consistently with the reality of the character and the character's world. Acting requires that all aspects of your self—your body, voice, thoughts, and feelings—be available, integrated, and controllable. They are the tools of your trade.

In the process of growing up, however, you may have begun to lose some of the natural wholeness and openness you enjoyed as a child. There may be some aspects of your body and voice, some forms of expression, some feelings, thoughts, and experiences that you have learned to ignore or suppress. For some of you, for example, touching and being touched in public may be uncomfortable at first. In this part, you will begin to rediscover your childlike wholeness and openness, as well as the natural ability for fantasy and for playing with others that you enjoyed as a child.

You can recapture all this best when you are *relaxed, playful,* and *nonjudgmental.* Some psychologists call this *the creative state,* and they say it happens when your internal "parent" allows your inner "child" to come out and play. The first and most important step toward this creative state is relaxation, which naturally leads to greater openness and responsiveness. In a relaxed state, you will find it easy to experience what we call *centeredness,* to begin moving and sounding in a more fully integrated and controllable way, to enter into a more free and open exchange of energy with your fellow workers, and to experience the multiple levels of reality that exist simultaneously in every performance situation. This will be the focus of the next four steps. They will introduce what is, for the professional actor, the work of a lifetime of physical, vocal, mental, and spiritual development.

5

Relaxing and Centering

For most of us, performing arouses anxiety. This can be both pleasurable (as in the quest for creative discovery) and painful (as in the fear of failure). In either case, this anxiety can make your muscles tense and disrupt your breathing and thinking. It also interferes with your ability to react; it "freezes" you and reduces your creativity. For all these reasons, tension is the greatest enemy of the creative state. For some, "stage fright" can become debilitating; the great British actor Sir Laurence Olivier suffered from it so badly at one point in his career that he had to stop acting for several years.

When you find yourself scared or stuck, you may attempt to compensate by trying harder, by putting more effort into the work and trying to force your way through it. Unfortunately, this is exactly the wrong thing to do. It only increases your tension and further reduces your freedom of creative response. It is common to see student actors make the mistake of trying too hard; the harder they try, the worse they get. This excessive effort makes them self-aware, obscures their own experience of their work, and reduces their control.

Think of trying to open a desk drawer that is stuck: if you tug at it with all your might, chances are that it will come loose all at once, fly open, and spill the contents. Because you were using excessive force, you failed to feel the exact moment when the drawer loosened, and you lost control. You weren't experiencing the drawer anymore; you were instead experiencing only *your own effort*. Too often, student actors make this same mistake in performance; they stop experiencing the scene and instead become aware of their own effort, and this can become their erroneous idea of the way it feels to act.

Unfortunately, many actors are driven to excessive effort by their fear of failure or their desire to please their audience. They feel unworthy of the audience's attention unless they do something extraordinary to earn it; the option of doing nothing, of simply allowing themselves to "be there," is terrifying. They feel naked and exposed and become desperate to do something, anything! As a result, they have difficulty experiencing what is really happening on stage.

Here is the secret that will make miracles happen for you as an actor: acting is mostly a matter of *letting go*. Letting go of too much effort, letting go of chronic physical tension, letting go of a false voice, letting go of your preconceptions about the work, letting go of fear, and, most of all, letting go of who you already are in order to become someone new. The first step in letting go is to *relax*.

Relaxation

Relaxation for the actor does not mean reduced energy or slackness; rather it means that all unnecessary tensions have been removed; the remaining energy has been purposefully focused and awareness is at a high level.

The kind of relaxation you want is a state in which you are most ready to react to the slightest stimulus, like the cat in front of the mouse hole. Although the cat is completely alert and in total readiness to spring, it is not tense. If it were tense, the tension in its muscles would slow down its reactions and make its movements awkward. The same is true of people.

The best description of the relaxed actor's state is what meditators call *restful alertness*. You are already capable of restful alertness; you don't need to do anything to achieve it; you only need to become still enough to experience it. Do this now, through a simple meditation.

EXERCISE 5.1: A MEDITATION

Sit comfortably in your chair, both feet flat on the floor, back and neck straight but not rigid, hands resting on your thighs. Look at a spot on the floor eight feet in front of you or, if you like, close your eyes. Focus your awareness on your breath flowing in and out of your nose. Allow any thoughts that come up to play across your consciousness, then simply return your awareness to your breath. Resist nothing. Sit for as long as you are comfortable. Whatever experience you have is correct.

The ability to relax can be learned. Psychologists speak of the "relaxation response" which develops with repetition just like any other skill. The following exercise is a classic in the field of relaxation. Although you can quickly learn it on your own, it would be useful for your teacher or a partner to lead at first so you aren't distracted by having to read the instructions. If necessary, a tape recording of these instructions with the necessary pauses would be useful.

EXERCISE 5.2: RELAXATION

Lie in a comfortable position, knees slightly raised. As in your meditation, your breath is the focus of your awareness. Imagine that each inhalation is a warm, energy-filled fluid flowing into your body. Each exhalation carries away with it tension and inhibition, like a refreshing wave. Breathe deeply and easily in a slow, natural, regular rhythm.

Each successive breath will be sent into a different part of the body. As the breath flows into each area, let the muscles there tighten as much as they can; then, as the breath flows out, the muscles release and the breath carries all the tension away with it, leaving the area refreshed and at ease. Exhaling is letting go.

The sequence of breaths will move from the top of the body downward. Increasingly, the regular rhythm of your breathing should make the muscular contractions and relaxations flow smoothly down the body like a slow wave. Send your breath into each area in turn:

1. The *forehead and scalp,* furrowing the brow, then releasing it; the eyes at rest, closed and turned slightly downward.
2. The *jaw,* clenching, then falling easily downward until the teeth are about one-half inch apart.
3. The *tongue,* extending, then lying easily in the mouth.
4. The *front of the neck,* with the chin extending down to touch the chest, stretching the back of the neck, then rolling the head easily back down.
5. The *back of the neck* with the top of the head rolling under to touch the floor, stretching the front of the neck, then rolling the head slowly down and lengthening the neck.
6. The *upper chest,* swelling outward in all directions so that the shoulders are widened, then easily subsiding, feeling the shoulder blades spread and melt into the floor, wider than before.
7. The *arms and hands,* becoming stiff and straight like steel rods; the hands clenching into fists, then easily uncurling and melting into the floor.
8. The *pit of the stomach,* clenching, becoming a small, hard ball, then, with a sigh, releasing.
9. The *knees,* stiffening as the legs straighten, the feet being pushed downward by this action, then releasing the legs and feeling them melt into the floor.
10. The *feet,* with the toes reaching up toward the eyes (but the heels remain on the floor), then releasing and falling into a natural position.
11. The *length of the body,* with the heels and the shoulder blades simultaneously pushing downward into the floor so that the whole body lifts upward in a long arch, then, with a sigh, slowly falling, the body lengthening as it relaxes, melting deep into the floor.

Now take ten deep, slow, regular breaths, and with each breath move more deeply into relaxation, remaining alert and refreshed. The flow of breath is a continuous cycle of energy that is stored comfortably in the body; with each breath, this store of energy is increased. If a yawn comes to you, enjoy it fully; vocalize the exhalation, letting the sound of the yawn pour out.

As you repeat this exercise on successive days, you can give yourself the instructions silently. Keep a steady rhythm that follows the tempo of deep, relaxed breathing. Gradually, the action of the exercise will become natural, and you will no longer need to think of the instructions, giving your full awareness to the flow of contractions and relaxations that follow the breath as it travels down the body like a wave, awakening, refreshing, and relaxing it, making you ready for work. Use this exercise as an easy and quick preparation for all future work. Over a period of time, it will help break up and dissolve chronic bundles of tension within your body.

Like any skill, relaxation must be developed over a period of time and maintained once achieved. Meditation and relaxation techniques are used by many actors throughout their lives.

Finding Center

In addition to learning to relax, you must also develop *wholeness*. Good acting requires that all the parts of your body, your voice, and your mind work together in an integrated way. This integration is a natural state. Even if, as you've grown up, you have learned habits of movement or voice that have made you unintegrated and awkward, you can easily rediscover your natural wholeness. You begin by experiencing the true source of integrated movement and voice deep in the center of your body.

This idea of a personal center is not just a metaphor; it has a tangible physical dimension. There is a "pure" center deep within the body, at your center of gravity, roughly three finger-widths below your navel. It is here that the breath (and therefore the voice) originates. All large motions of the body and all your deepest impulses also originate here. The pure center is the undistorted condition from which we begin our work so we may develop the unique ways of using the body and voice required by the character we will create throughout the rest of our working process.

Here is an exercise to help you develop a specific sense of your physical center.

EXERCISE 5.3: FINDING CENTER

Stand upright and relax. Clear your mind and witness your body as it performs the following activities:

1. Move either foot out to the side about two feet; rock from foot to foot, feeling your center of gravity moving from side to side. Quickly make your rocking motions smaller and smaller, like a bowling pin that almost falls down; come to rest on center.
2. Move either foot forward about two feet; make front-to-back rocking motions and again come to rest on center.
3. Move your center around rotationally, exploring the limits of various stances. Feel the weight of your body flowing out of your center, through the legs, and into the ground.
4. With one finger, point at the spot in your body that you feel is your center; don't be concerned about where it "ought" to be; sense where it really is.
5. Explore how your center is involved in breathing, making sound, and moving.

You may have found that your center is not at the "pure" location just below your navel. Many of us have lost touch with this natural center and operate instead from some higher center, such as our chests, or even our heads.

Unfortunately, when we fail to work from our pure center, we inevitably look and sound stiff and superficial, and our movements and voice will not have the fullness and expressiveness needed for performance. If you need to, repeat this exercise over a period of days and weeks, letting your sense of center drop until the pure center starts to feel natural to you.

My friend Cicely Berry of the RSC says that the center is where laughter begins. Developing your sense of physical center will help you to develop a psychological and spiritual centeredness as well, because at this deep level your energy exists simultaneously in physical, psychological, and spiritual forms.

As you become aware of your center over a period of days, you will notice that it moves within your body as your mood changes; frequently, your center will rise upward when you are in an excited or fearful state, or downward in states of well-being or determination. You will notice, too, that different people have different characteristic centers and that the locations of their centers are very appropriate to their personalities. Such diversity can be found in people who have a "lot of guts," who "follow their nose," "lead with their chins," are "all heart," "drag their feet," "have their heads in the clouds," and so on. Therefore, although we begin our work from our ideal center, there is no "correct" voice or posture for a performance until these are determined by the demands of the role.

Summary of Step 5

For most of us, performing arouses anxiety. This makes us tense, interferes with our ability to react, and reduces our creativity. For all these reasons, tension is the greatest enemy of the creative state, so the first step toward a creative state and is to relax. When we speak of relaxation for the actor, we do not mean the ordinary sense of reduced energy or slackness, but rather, a state in which all unnecessary tensions have been removed, energy has been purposefully focused, and awareness is at a high level. This is what meditators call "restful alertness."

Besides being relaxed, you also need to be *whole*, because good acting requires that all the parts of your body, your voice, and your mind work together in an integrated way. The true source of integrated movement and voice is deep within the center of your body. This "pure" center is roughly three finger-widths below your navel. It is here that your breath (and therefore your voice), as well as laughter, all large motions of the body, and all your deepest impulses originate. The pure center is an undistorted condition from which we may begin our work and develop in any way required by the role. Eventually, we will find the center appropriate to the character.

STEP

6 Breathing, Sounding, and Moving from Center

The relaxation exercise (5.2) focuses on the breath for a very good reason: breath is life. The word *psychology* means "study of the soul," and the word for soul, *psyche*, originally meant "vital breath." Think about it: when you breathe, you are bringing the outside world into your body, then sending it out again. Your breath constantly reflects your relationship to your world. When you are frightened, you hold your breath because you don't want to let the threatening world in. When you are happy, your breath flows freely. The way you feel about your world is expressed in the way you breathe it in and breathe it out.

This is why your natural voice, which is based on your breath, is so expressive of your inner state. You can see sobbing, laughing, gasping, sighing, and all the other sounds you make as the natural and automatic reflections of your relationship to your world. Your voice so completely reflects your inner state that sounding and speaking literally turns you inside out.

This is why actors are careful not to force their voices into unnatural and artificial patterns and often work hard to free their natural voices from bad habits. Unfortunately, television has turned many of us into "talking heads," causing us to lose touch with the natural breathing that begins deep inside our bodies. Here is an exercise that will help you to experience the natural integration of breath and voice.

EXERCISE 6.1: BREATHING AND SOUNDING FROM CENTER

1. Sit comfortably in your chair or lie on the floor. Relax yourself by allowing the breath to sweep through your body as in the relaxation exercise (5.2). As you breathe easily and slowly, become aware that your breath is rising and falling from a deep place in your body, a little below your navel.
2. As your breath travels outward from this deep place, make sound lightly; do not disturb your breath, just allow it to vibrate, as it may sometimes do just as you are falling asleep. This is your natural voice—your vibrating breath carrying energy from deep within you into the outside world.

3. Reach effortlessly with your vibrating breath into the world around you. Put yourself, at random, into new positions and experience the vibrating breath flowing through each. What changes occur in the voice?

4. As you continue to produce sound, feel the vibrations of that sound spreading into every part of your body: out of the neck, into the head and chest; into the back, the stomach, the buttocks; into the arms and hands; into the legs and feet; and into the scalp. Feel the sound radiating from every part of your body. With a light fingertip touch, check every surface of your body. Are there "dead spots" that are not participating in the sound?

Examine your experience during sounding: did you have a new sense of the capacity of your entire body to join in the act of sounding? Did you feel more in touch with yourself and with the space around you, as if your sound were literally reaching outside yourself in a tangible way? Are you now more alert, refreshed, and relaxed?

You have begun to experience how physical, vocal, and mental qualities are integral to one another, because the body, voice, and mind are all integral to one another, and the breath is the great unifier that binds them together.

The Cycle of Energy

Whenever we try to do something, to achieve some objective—whenever we *act*—we send energy flowing out from our centers into the outer world in the form of sound, speech, gesture, or movement. Usually, our action provokes a reaction from someone, and we receive the new energy of this reaction through seeing, hearing, or touching. This new energy flows into us and touches our center, which in turn elicits a further reaction from us, and so on. As you learned in Step 3, it is this flow of *interactions* that makes the play unfold. As we have said, *acting is reacting*, and the cycle of energy that flows out of us and back into us makes this happen. (This important process will be explored in greater detail in Part Four.)

This idea of a cycle of energy is central to the Asian martial arts, such as *tai chi chuan*, and study in these arts can be of great benefit to the actor. Here is an exercise taken from yoga that will let you experience the cycle of energy (see Figure 6.1).

EXERCISE 6.2: THE CYCLE OF ENERGY

Sit on the floor with your back straight, and spread your legs a little with the knees slightly raised. Feel lifted from your center out of the top of your head so that your back and neck are long and wide. The head is level, eyes are ahead, and the waist is level as well.

1. Breathing out, reach forward and down with your arms and torso, keeping your back and neck long and your shoulders wide. Imagine yourself in a large theater, bowing to someone sitting in the last row.

2. As you begin to breathe in, use your arms and hands to gather your breath into the lower part of your body, scooping "energy" into the funnel formed by your legs.

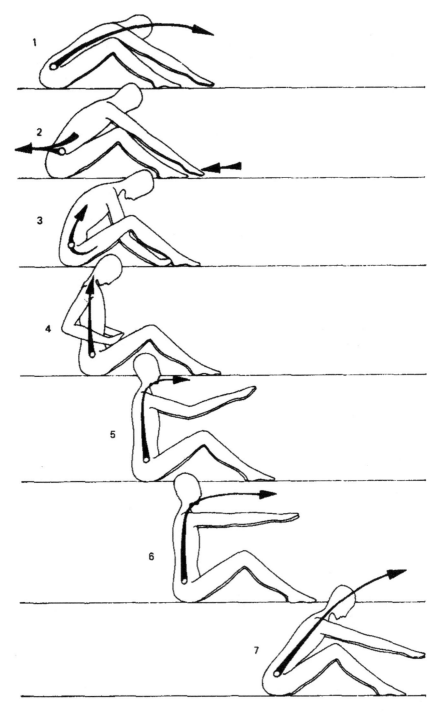

FIGURE 6.1   The Cycle of Energy.

3. As the breath begins to fill you, feel its warmth and power flowing up within you. Follow its upward movement with your hands.

4. As the breath rises in your body, it lifts you, straightening and lengthening the upper torso and neck, lifting the head, widening the shoulders and the throat as it flows upward like a wave moving you in a slow undulation. You unfurl like a fern opening.

5. The breath then flows into the outer world; give an "ah" sound to that imaginary person sitting at the back of the theater and accompany it with an unfolding gesture of the arms toward the person.

6. As the power of the breath begins to diminish, close your mouth so the "ah" sound becomes an "oh" and then an "m," and you experience a tingling sensation in your mouth and nose areas. The smooth flow of the sound produces a trisyllable word, "ah-oh-m," or *om*.

7. As the breath and sound die away, your body again bows forward and down, your arms reach forward to scoop in a new quantity of breath energy, and the cycle begins again.

8. Repeat the cycle several times, feeling the continuity of inward and outward breaths so the entire exercise becomes one unbroken, flowing experience with no sharp corners.

You have begun to experience the cycle of energy within yourself. Next you will begin to explore your connection with others, for it is in the interactions between you and your partners that the action of drama truly lives.

Your Relationship to Gravity

You experience your center in specific relationship to gravity, and you move and sound within that relationship. The way you experience gravity, like your breathing, is a fundamental expression of your relationship to your world. Some days, it seems that we wake up heavier, with "the weight of the world" on our shoulders, and we feel "down"; at the saddest times we say we have a "heavy heart." On the other hand, sometimes we feel "up" or "light-hearted." When we are sure of ourselves, we feel as if we are receiving strength from gravity, and we speak of "knowing where we stand," or "holding our ground."

People's attitudes toward gravity can be seen in their postures. When Arthur Miller opens his play *Death of a Salesman* with Willy Loman crossing the stage, back bent under the weight of his sample case, Willy's sense of defeat and hopelessness are directly expressed in the way he is losing his fight with gravity. In the musical theater, in contrast, it is a convention that lovers actually defy gravity by skipping, as if they were about to float away "on cloud nine."

Here is an exercise to help you discover the various ways in which you experience gravity.

EXERCISE 6.3: ROOTS

Imagine yourself standing on a mirror. Below you is your other self with its own center; imagine a bond between your center "up here" and the one "down there" in your mirror image. This imaginary bond of energy is like a root. As you move, your root moves with you; you can even "detach" your root. Try the following movements; don't act them out, simply experience them through these images and discover what they feel like.

1. Select a destination; detach and lift your root, move to the destination, and replant your root there.
2. Now move to a destination without lifting your root, plowing a furrow through the ground as you move. Feel yourself pushing your whole body through space. We will call this *molding*.
3. Now lift your root and leave it dangling the whole time, whether moving or standing still. We will call this *floating*.
4. Now imagine the root being drawn upward, still attached at your center, but now lifting your center upward and out of the top of your head. Move with the sense that you have to reach down to touch the floor: you are *flying*.

There is a distinct difference between the experiences of molding, floating, and flying, though each of them might express several different things: molding, for instance, can feel like dejection or defeat, but it might also feel like determination or commitment; floating can feel like joy or enthusiasm, but it might also feel like confusion or vulnerability. The particular emotional quality of any one of these states is determined only by the context created by the play.

Begin to observe in everyday life how the position of people's bodily centers and their relationships to gravity express their characters and moods. Record your observations in your journal, perhaps with sketches.

Phrasing Movement

In the previous exercise you began to move through space by "lifting" your rooted center, moving, then "planting" your rooted center again at your destination. Review this experience; did it give you a heightened sense of clarity and purposefulness in your movements? Did the exercise make you more aware of the *shape* of your movements?

Stanislavski said that "everything that happens on a stage should have a definite purpose"; this includes stage movement. When an actor moves on stage, he or she is moving for a definite purpose; that movement is an action, driven by some objective that is usually in relation to the other characters; for example, he or she may be *approaching* other characters, either in a positive way (like persuading, imploring, or embracing them) or a negative way (like threatening or attacking

them). Alternatively, he or she may be *avoiding* or *retreating* from another character in fear, or disgust, or respect. Whatever the quality of the movement, it is an
active expression of action and relationship.

You will find that when you are in action, you will naturally feel impulses to
move appropriately to your action, and these impulses generate what we call the
blocking of the scene; blocking is the physical expression of the action of the scene
expressed in changing spatial relationships (more on this in Step 16).

Whatever causes it, good stage movement must have clarity and well-
defined shape. In good writing or speaking, thoughts are shaped into phrases
and sentences, each with a clear shape that is essential to good communication.
Just so, your stage movement needs to be organized and shaped into clear
phraseology.

EXERCISE 6.4: PHRASING MOVEMENT

As in Exercise 6.3, begin by "seeing" your own rooted center in relationship to your
mirror image beneath the floor. Now make a movement by following each of these
steps:

1. Think of a specific destination.
2. Begin to move by lifting the root; exaggerate this motion at first.
3. Carry your root to your destination and "land" there.
4. As you land, "spear" your root into the floor to complete your movement.
5. Repeat this action several times, paying special attention to the sense of beginning, middle, and end to each movement phrase.
6. Now begin to play with variations of this cycle, extending them beyond realistic
   movement. For instance, try lifting the root slowly and heavily, then drag it to
   the destination and dump it there so that it "plops" into the ground. Or make
   your lift light and high, moving away from your destination, then throw your
   root toward your destination and fly there, landing with a light jump. Invent
   other patterns and qualities of movement, but in each case keep a clear sense of
   the beginning, middle, and end of each movement.

Notice also that when you are *not* moving, you are grounded and still.
Avoid "wandering" unless it is appropriate to your action (for instance, if your
character is confused and desperate) although even then this must be expressed
in a clear and purposeful way. Beginning actors often have difficulty standing
still; they tend to rock from foot to foot, or wander aimlessly. This is a natural
expression of uncertainty and discomfort, their lack of clear purpose on the
stage. Conversely, some beginning actors manifest their anxiety by "locking
up" so rigidly that they are unable to react readily. Avoid both extremes. Learn
to stand still, and yet be ready to move. When you do move, make your movements economical and purposeful, clearly shaped with a beginning, middle,
and end.

Summary of Step 6

When you breathe, you are bringing the outside world into your body, then sending it out again. Your breath constantly reflects your relationship to your world. This is why your natural voice, based on your breath, is the way you literally turn yourself inside out.

As you learned in Step 3, it is the flow of *interactions* that makes the play unfold. Acting is reacting, and the cycle of energy flowing out of us and back into us makes this possible.

You experience your center in specific relationship to gravity, and you move and sound within that relationship, so the way you experience gravity, like your breathing, is also a fundamental expression of your relationship to your world. Three of the ways we experience gravity can be called molding, floating, and flying.

Stage movement is a physical expression of action. It must be clearly shaped, with the same kind of phraseology as any good kind of expression, with a clear beginning, middle, and end.

S T E P

7 Collaboration

Actors always collaborate, literally "labor together," with others, whether in a stage play, TV show, or film. They work not only with other actors, but also with directors, stage managers, costume and make-up people, and many others. The success of any collaborative artistic endeavor depends on the ability of these many kinds of artists to work together toward the common goal of bringing the material to life.

When a group works together in the best possible way, the energy of each member of the group flows into a common stream, forming one energy that is greater than the sum of its parts. Everyone on the team receives more energy from the group than they give to it. No member of the team needs to sacrifice individuality; rather, each member finds his or her individual power enhanced by membership in the group.

Such ideal teamwork is achieved only when five conditions have been met:

1. When each member is genuinely *committed* to being a member of the team
2. When each member *supports* the work of the others
3. When there is *trust* and *mutual respect* within the team
4. When all agree to maintain free and open *communication*
5. When the efforts of all are in *alignment* toward the common purpose

Let's examine each of these points.

1. *Commitment.* It is part of your responsibility as an actor to be committed on five levels at once:
    a. To *your own talent*, to being as good as you can be and continually learning to be better.
    b. To each *role* you play, to finding the truth of the character and of each moment in the performance.
    c. To each *ensemble* of which you are a member, to contributing to the success and growth of everyone in it.
    d. To each piece of *material* you perform, to finding and expressing the truth it contains.
    e. To your *audience* and the *world* you serve through your work.

2. *Support for Your Partners.* We all have different reasons for working in the theater or film, but we support each other's objectives, even if we do not share them. We assume a nonjudgmental attitude.
3. *Trust and Mutual Respect.* We respect other workers as a matter of principle; we treat them exactly as we would want to be treated ourselves. We trust each of our partners to do their jobs, and even if we disagree with their methods, we do our best to accept and utilize their contributions. If this eventually proves to be impossible, we seek resolution through respectful but honest and direct communication.
4. *Free and Open Communication.* No matter how supportive, trustful, and respectful we all are, creative collaboration is difficult and we are bound to encounter differences of opinion, conflicting needs, and artistic challenges. All these problems can become opportunities for creativity as long as we can communicate freely and reasonably about them.
5. *Alignment.* When every member of the team shares a common purpose, each is free to work in his or her own way and still contribute to the overall effort. People with very different artistic methods, as well as different political, religious, cultural, and artistic values, can work in alignment toward the common purpose as long as the common purpose is well understood by all and the other four conditions listed here have been met.

Commitment, support, trust, respect, communication, and *alignment:* these are the cornerstones of teamwork, and they all require that you keep your attention on the job at hand and *park your ego at the rehearsal room door.* Here are four enjoyable exercises which explore these qualities on a literal, physical level.

EXERCISE 7.1: FALLING

1. Everybody picks a partner. Stand three feet behind your partner with one foot back for stability (see Figure 7.1). By mutual agreement, your partner starts to fall backward, keeping the body straight but not stiff. Catch your partner right away, and gently raise him or her back up.
2. Your partner falls only a short way at first, and then gradually falls farther and farther, until he or she falls about four feet above the floor. If your partner becomes frightened, reassure him or her.
3. Reverse roles and repeat.

Caution: Do not attempt this exercise unless you are confident of being able to catch your partner; otherwise, serious injury could result.

EXERCISE 7.2: FLOATING

1. Form groups of seven or nine. One person from each group becomes the "floater." The floaters lie flat, close their eyes, and fold their arms across their

FIGURE 7.1   Falling Exercise.

chests. The others kneel beside them, three or four on either side, and prepare to lift them (see Figure 7.2A).

2. Everyone begins to breathe in unison. When a group breathing rhythm is established, *gently and slowly* lift the floaters, keeping them perfectly level. Those being lifted should feel as if they are floating.
3. Lift the floaters as high as the group can reach while keeping them level (see Figure 7.2B).
4. Slowly lower the floaters, rocking them gently back and forth, like a leaf settling to earth.
5. Repeat with each member of the group.

Now let's use our collaborative skills to create a group scene.

EXERCISE 7.3: TUG OF WAR

1. Each member of the group creates—in pantomime—a piece of rope about two feet long.
2. Standing in a single long line, each of you "attaches" your rope to those on either side, so the group creates one long rope.
3. Now separate at the center and slide down the rope until two teams are formed.
4. Have a tug of war. Don't let the rope stretch or break. Continue until one team wins.

This exercise is a good example of performance reality: the rope ceases to be real if any members of the group fail to make their parts real and connected to the whole. This requires that *every individual actor must believe in the whole rope.* This is a good metaphor for the saying "There are no small parts, only small actors." The total reality of the show depends on every element in it.

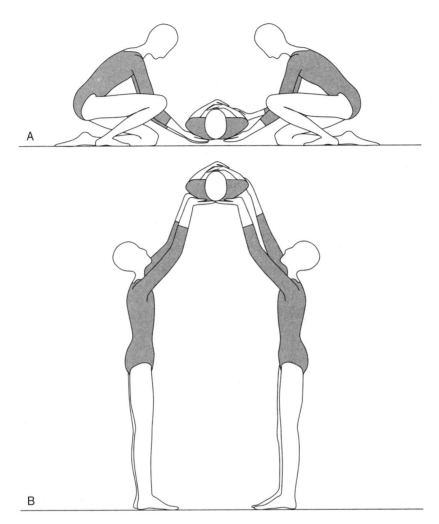

FIGURE 7.2   Floating Exercise.

Our concluding group exercise will illustrate the results of unconditional teamwork.

EXERCISE 7.4: GROUP LEVITATION

1. Stand in one large, perfectly round circle, facing inward. Each of you puts your arms around the waists of the persons on either side (see Figure 7.3).
2. Start to breathe in unison. Bend your knees slightly when exhaling, then lift the person on either side as you breathe in. Do not lift yourself; lift those you are holding, and allow yourself to be lifted by them.

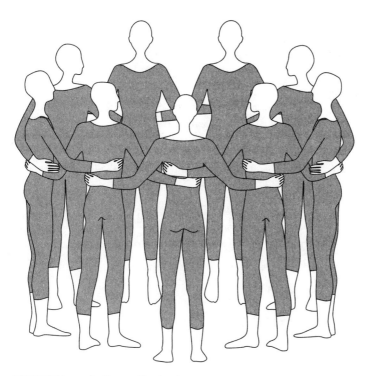

FIGURE 7.3 A Group Levitation.

3. As you breathe out, say the word "higher," and try to lift those you are holding
    higher and higher. Allow the rhythm of the group to accelerate naturally until
    you all *leave the ground.*

Do you see how this exercise symbolizes the way we work together? When
the energy of every member of the group is connected to the common goal and there
is a basis of mutual trust, respect, and open communication, the result is greater
than the sum of its parts: everyone gets more energy back than he or she gives!

Seeing and Hearing

In Step 2 you learned that a story moves toward a dramatic conclusion as energy
passes from character to character through a series of interactions that form the
scenes of the play or film. The continuity and strength of this flow of energy is
what gives the story its momentum, which in acting we call *pace*. If the flow is
interrupted for any reason, the momentum is broken, and the evolving drama
stalls, causing a drop in dramatic tension and suspense.

Actors usually, and correctly, focus their attention on the energy they *send*
to the other actors, moment by moment, through the actions of their character

directed outward toward the other characters. It is equally important, however, that each actor *receive* the energy from the other actors that provokes each action (again, acting is reacting). If an actor reacts only to his or her premeditated idea of what they are "supposed" to be receiving from the other actor, instead of what they are really getting, the flow of the scene will not be a real event.

Actors receive energy, of course, through seeing and hearing one another. Moreover, drama involves circumstances in which the stakes are raised and what the characters get from one another has special significance; seeing and hearing on stage must therefore be more acute than in real life.

One way to experience such heightened perception is to think of yourself as a camera that is recording everything you see and hear on stage. This is not just a metaphor; an audience does in fact tend to mimic the seeing and hearing of the actor; when you focus intently on a particular detail on stage, for example, the audience feels as if they are seeing that detail in a close-up. You literally act as a camera for your audience.

Here is an enjoyable exercise that will give you the experience of this significant seeing and hearing.

EXERCISE 7.5: CAMERA GAME

Repeat your simple action scene (Exercise 2.3) or some simple activity like bowling. You and your partner will take turns being the "camera," and your teacher or someone else will call out randomly when you will switch. The actor being the camera at any given moment will take the most interesting pictures possible, and is free to move in any way the camera might move, zooming in for close-ups, panning across the scene, cutting from one angle to another, and so on.

After the exercise, discuss the scene. Was your hearing and seeing of one another heightened? Did being focused on being the camera give you greater freedom from self-awareness? Were you more in action as the camera? Do you see why having a meaningful and active objective (in this case taking pictures) is so effective?

Pursuing an Objective

In the camera exercise, you probably discovered that you benefited from having the objective of taking pictures as the camera, and that this objective and the action it produced made you see and hear your partner with greater significance and acuteness. It also gave you a focus of attention that relaxed you, made you less self-aware, and more playful.

As you learned in Step 2, action is the means whereby your character pursues an objective in order to satisfy a need. This process flows through every interaction between the characters as the scene unfolds. It is essential to the flow of the scene that all the actors are not only in action themselves, but receiving the actions of one another. Again, acting is reacting, and your ability to receive your partner's energy through perception is the necessary starting point of your action.

EXERCISE 7.6: GUARD AND THIEF

In this game, you and your partner are both blindfolded, or simply keep your eyes closed. One of you is the "guard," the other is a "thief." The thief has the objective of crossing the room and touching the far wall; the guard has the objective of stopping the thief by touching him or her. When the thief is touched by the guard, he or she "dies." At first, the guard is defensive, reacting to the thief, who tries various strategies to get past the guard; when the teacher calls "attack," the guard goes on the attack and seeks out the thief, who tries to elude capture.

Discuss this exercise. How did raising the stakes heighten perception and enhance the drama of the game? Did you experience the difference between the active and passive forms of action each character used in the different versions of the game? Did suspense increase when the game lasted longer?

Summary of Step 7

Actors always work in a group situation. The success of the process depends on the ability of everyone to work together toward the common goal of bringing the material to life. When a group works together in the best possible way, the energy of each member of the group flows into a common stream, forming one energy that is greater than the sum of its parts. Such ideal teamwork is achieved only when five conditions have been met: first, when each member is genuinely *committed* to being a member of the team; second, when each member *supports* the work of the others; third, when that support is founded on *trust and mutual respect;* fourth, when all agree to maintain free and open *communication;* and fifth, when the efforts of each member is in *alignment* toward the common purpose. When all these conditions have been met, each member of the group is empowered to do his or her best work, and each gets more energy from the group than he or she gives to it.

The connection between actors through which the energy of the scene flows depends on the ability of each actor to receive, through significant hearing, seeing, touching, and so on. The real interactions between actors created in this way give you a strong focus of attention that helps to reduce self-awareness and thereby promotes creativity.

8 Entering the Actor's State of Mind

Stanislavski tells of an acting student who, like many of us, suffered from stage fright. He became tense and distracted on stage because he was overly aware of being watched. One day, his teacher gave him the simple task of counting the floorboards on the stage. The student soon became totally engrossed in this task. When he finished, he realized that it was the first time he had been on stage without self-consciousness. Surprisingly to him, the experience was liberating and exhilarating. Stanislavski points out that it was the student's total focus on his task that had truly allowed him to forget about being watched. He was *fully in action* and therefore became unself-conscious.

Public Solitude

From this experience, Stanislavski developed his principle of the "dramatic task," or the *objective*. Instead of counting floorboards, you focus your full awareness on what your character is trying to achieve at any given moment. When you become so engrossed in these objectives that your self-consciousness is greatly reduced, you have achieved the condition Stanislavski called *public solitude*.

Public solitude is the ability to experience yourself as though you were in private, even though you are in public. We can see public solitude in real life: an athlete making a play in front of millions of spectators is aware only of the play and may "forget" the spectators entirely. You have probably seen people driving their cars on the freeways who are so engrossed in their fantasies that they are doing extraordinarily private things even though hundreds of people are driving past them. You yourself at times have been so engrossed in what you were doing that you forgot you were in public.

People who are fully in action are automatically in public solitude. The actor who is totally focused on the character's objective can forget that an audience or a camera is watching. It is at such moments of public solitude that self-consciousness and fear are conquered.

Dual Consciousness

There is a danger in public solitude, however. Some young actors tend to focus so much on the solitude that they begin to ignore the requirements of being in public. They try to achieve some sort of trancelike state in which they lose artistic control and their sense of performance. Public solitude is not like a trance. Like the athlete, you remain in control, fully aware of your task, and even though you have "forgotten" about the spectators or the camera, they are still in the background of your awareness.

This, then, is the question: can you be completely engrossed in the action and world of your character and simultaneously be aware of the demands of performance, making the artistic choices required to express your action in a public form worthy of your audience's or the camera's attention?

This question is answered by your capacity for *dual consciousness*, your ability to function on more than one level of awareness at a time. As one of Stanislavski's students put it after a successful performance:

> I divided myself, as it were, into two personalities. One continued as [the character], the other was an observer [the actor]. Strangely enough this duality not only did not impede, it actually promoted my creative work. It encouraged and lent impetus to it.[1]

The two levels of consciousness, then, are that of the *character* pursuing his or her objective and that of the *actor* observing and adjusting the performance for the sake of the spectators or the camera.

Different performance situations may require more or less emphasis on one level of consciousness or the other. In television sketch comedy, for instance, we may allow a bit more of the actor awareness to be present in the performance (this is why stand-up comedians are often successful in television sitcoms even though they may not be very skillful actors in the characterizational sense). In naturalistic stage plays, however, we strive to reduce our actor consciousness to the minimum. For serious dramatic work for the camera, the actor must be completely invisible, leaving only the character behind. In fact, we say that the camera requires "no acting" at all. Even in this case, however, you do not lose your actor consciousness completely, nor do you want to. If you did, you would lose your ability to make artistic choices.

Dual consciousness may sound difficult, but it is really a very natural ability. When you were a child, a puddle easily became a vast ocean, but it didn't need to stop being a puddle: you hadn't learned yet that something isn't supposed to be two different things at once, and that we aren't supposed to be in

---

[1]Stanislavski, *An Actor's Handbook*, trans. and ed. Elizabeth Reynolds Hapgood (New York: Theatre Arts Books, 1936), p. 9. Copyright © 1936, 1961, 1963 by Elizabeth Reynolds Hapgood.

two different realities at the same time. As an actor, you will have to forget your adult logic and allow yourself to rediscover this childhood ability to make believe, to joyfully enter the world of fantasy.

Many actors say that they chose acting as a career specifically because it gives them a chance to use their imaginations in the most complete way possible. Patrick Stewart, best known as Captain Picard on *Star Trek: The Next Generation* (and who is also a great Shakespearean actor), once told me, "What first attracted me to acting was the fantasy world of the theater into which I could escape from the much less pleasant world of my childhood." Another great actor, Sir Alec Guinness, spoke of acting as a way to escape from "my dreary old life."

EXERCISE 8.1: MAKING BELIEVE

Repeat the simple task exercise (2.1), but this time give yourself a character and a dramatic situation that raises the stakes. If your task was to build a house of cards, perhaps you are a condemned man about to be executed, waiting for the governor to phone with your pardon. See if you can relax and accept the character's reality. Are you able to hold the dual awareness of your character's world and your actor's concerns?

Indicating

Acting students commonly do too much on stage. They are afraid that it is not enough to simply do what their characters are doing; they also try to embellish, to show us how the characters feel, or what kind of people they are. They posture, exaggerate their emotions, use excessive gestures and facial expressions, and take on a false voice. Their performance is saying something like, "Hey, look at how angry I am," or "Look at what a villain I am."

This excessive behavior is called *indicating*. You are indicating when you are *showing* the audience something about the character instead of simply *doing* what the character does. Actors indicate for various reasons. Some feel unworthy of the audience's attention and think they have to work hard to earn it; some indicate because they are afraid of losing control over the performance; others simply think it "feels" the way they think acting should feel.

No matter the reason, indicating spoils the performance for the audience. It is part of the fun for the spectators to figure out for themselves how the characters feel and what kind of people they are by interpreting their actions. If instead you provide this information for them by indicating, you have created a performance *about* the character instead of presenting the character itself. The audience may get the message, but they won't feel involved.

Since indicating is often the result of trying to do too much, economy of performance can help you to avoid it. Stanislavski often encouraged his actors to "cut eighty percent"; to distill a performance to its essence, you must evaluate each element of the performance, retaining only that which contributes directly to a truthful expression of the character's action. As we often say, "Less is more," but of course it must be the correct "less."

Even after you have created a truthful moment, in rehearsal or performance, another form of indicating may befall you when you attempt to recreate that success in subsequent performances. Instead of having the courage to go back to the beginning and re-experience the entire process that produced the successful moment, you may be tempted instead to "play the result" and recreate the external form without reliving the internal process. This is a special danger in long runs of plays, or in repeated takes in filming, when actors have to perform the same scene over and over again.

The essence of good acting, then, is to do what the character does, completely and with the precise qualities required *as if for the first time and without adding anything superfluous.* Your job is to present the truthful evidence of the character's living action and leave the judgment and interpretation to the audience.

It is likely that you were guilty of some indicating when you were making believe in the previous exercise. You can learn to recognize indicating and avoid it by surrendering fully to your action. When you catch yourself *showing*, get back to *doing*. Repeat the previous exercise with this in mind.

EXERCISE 8.2: INDICATING

Repeat the making believe exercise (8.1), but this time ask your audience to signal by making some sort of noise whenever they feel that you are indicating. Compare their feedback with your own sense of being in action. Did you know when you were indicating? How strong is your impulse to *show* instead of *do*, or to do too much?

Discipline

The most important quality of mind a good actor can possess is the one that will most determine long-term growth and effectiveness: *discipline.*

Real discipline is not a matter of following someone else's rules. In the best sense, it is your acceptance of responsibility for your own development through systematic effort. You accept this responsibility not to please someone else, not to earn a grade, or a good review, or a job, but because you choose to become all that you can be.

Discipline is rooted in your *respect* for yourself, as well as your respect for your fellow workers, for your work, and for the world you serve through that work. Poor discipline is really a way of saying, "I'm not worth it" or "what I do doesn't matter." Discipline will come naturally if you can acknowledge your own value, the importance and seriousness of your work, and the great need for your work in the world.

Discipline also involves *regularity*. Your work, especially on technical skills, must be a daily affair. Stanislavski, looking back late in his life, had this to say:

> Let someone explain to me why the violinist who plays in an orchestra on the tenth violin must daily perform hour-long exercises or lose his power to play? Why does the dancer work daily over every muscle in his body? . . . And why may the dramatic artist do nothing, spend his day in coffee houses and hope for the gift [of inspiration] in the evening.[2]

Patience and a sense of striving together, being willing to accept the momentary failure for the sake of the long-term success—these are the attitudes you must nurture. The pressures of our educational system and of performance itself work against these attitudes, as does the normal desire of all of us to succeed. Resist these pressures. Enjoy your freedom as a student to explore a variety of approaches and experiences. Enjoy the journey, the exploration itself.

Summary of Step 8

When you are totally focused on your dramatic task, you lose self-consciousness and undue awareness of the audience. Stanislavski called this *public solitude*. However, you never totally lose awareness of the performance; rather you are able to operate on two levels simultaneously, the level of the character and his or her needs and world, and the level of the actor making artistic choices. This essential ability is called *dual consciousness*. Different kinds of performance require different emphasis on these two levels of consciousness.

Beginning actors often do too much; instead of simply doing what the characters do, they think they need to show the audience how the characters feel or what kind of people they are. When you *show* instead of *do*, you are *indicating*, and you lose the economy of a truthful performance. The audience may understand, but they won't believe or feel involved.

An actor's long-tern growth depends most on discipline, regular systematic effort rooted in self-respect, and the willingness to risk short-term failure for the sake of long-term success.

Summary of Part Two

The creative state requires playfulness and relaxation; tension and excessive effort disrupt our ability to react and invent. The actor must learn to let go of premeditations and physical tension and enter into the state of purposeful

---

[2] Constantin Stanislavski, *My Life in Art*, trans. J. J. Robbins (New York: Theatre Arts Books, 1952). Copyright © 1924 by Little, Brown & Co., and 1952 by Elizabeth Reynolds Hapgood.

relaxation which can be called *restful alertness*. In this relaxed state, you learn to operate from the deep center of your body. Working from this undistorted center gives you unity and rhythm; you then experiment to find the center and quality of energy appropriate to the role.

Your breath, voice, and large movements originate in your deep center. Your energy travels toward the outside world as breath, sound, or movement, all of which reflect your inner world. Operating in this way, you literally turn yourself inside out as energy flows out of you and provokes a reaction in the outside world, which you then receive. This cycle of giving and receiving forms the interactions that move the story of the play forward.

All this is experienced within the field of gravity, and your relationship to gravity is a fundamental expression of your relationship to the world. Entering into the character's action can inspire in you an experience of gravity, a center, and a quality of energy that is fundamental and unique to the role.

For the actor, this process of discovery always occurs within a group context. Teamwork is best achieved when everyone is *committed, supportive, trustful* and *respectful, open*, and *aligned* toward the common purpose. When these conditions have been met, every member of the group receives more energy from the group than they give to it, and the whole becomes greater than the sum of its parts.

Your focus on your objective allows you to become so engrossed in your action that you achieve *public solitude* and reduce self-consciousness, while your childlike ability for *dual consciousness* allows your awareness to be simultaneously on your character's objective and on your artistic concerns as an actor. Finally, we say that your job is to do what the character does, completely and as if for the first time, with the precise qualities required, not to *show* us the character or his or her feelings by *indicating*. You work toward all these goals with *discipline*, regular, systematic effort that risks short-term failure for the sake of long-term growth.

With the experiences you have had so far, you are now ready to begin work on an actual role. The next step is to learn to read the script in a way that motivates and guides your work; that will be the business of Part Three.

PART THREE

Preparing to Rehearse: Analyzing the Script

You are now ready to begin work on a role in a play. As the first step in your working process, you will make an early *analysis* of your lines and scene. This is the purpose of the next three steps. It is important that you understand that this analysis is only a *preparation* for actual rehearsal and not a substitute for it: analysis is not the creation of a blueprint which is merely filled in later. Rather, your initial analysis is intended to *inspire* and *guide* your exploration in rehearsal. It will point in the direction you will go, but it will not determine the ultimate destination. The actual performance will be discovered only gradually throughout your rehearsal process, when you will begin to experience the give-and-take of the living event that will grow between you and your fellow workers. This process will be explored in Part Four.

Selecting Your Scene

In the remaining steps it will be essential for you to apply what you learn to a scene of your own. First, team up with a partner, and together choose a two-character scene that will serve you both well. Your scene may come from a stage play, film, or television script. Since you don't want to burden yourselves with technical problems, such as handling difficult language or playing age, keep in mind the following qualities when selecting a scene:

1. Choose a *realistic* and *contemporary* scene, written in language that is comfortable to you.
2. Choose characters *close to you* in age and body type.
3. Select a *short* scene that can be read aloud in no more than five minutes; if necessary do only a section of a longer scene.
4. Best of all, choose a scene that *touches* you personally in some way.

There are many helpful anthologies of plays, films, TV scripts, and scenes for student actors. A list of useful plays and scene anthologies appears in Appendix B. Whatever the source of your scene, however, it is very important that you read the entire play or script from which the scene comes so you and your partner have all the necessary information about your characters and their functions.

Example Scenes

As we examine each step in the acting process, I will provide examples taken from five sources: Arthur Miller's *Death of a Salesman*, Tennessee Williams's *The Glass Menagerie*, Lorraine Hansberry's *A Raisin in the Sun*, Luis Valdez's *Zoot Suit*, and an episode of the television show *Cheers* by Tom Reeder.

My examples will be much more useful to you if you read these plays in their entirety at the outset (the script for the *Cheers* episode in Appendix B is not available). They are available in libraries and bookstores, in paperback, and in many anthologies. All the plays were also made as feature films and are available on video. The best of several film versions of *The Glass Menagerie*, made in 1987, was directed by Paul Newman and starred Joanne Woodward and John Malkovich. *A Raisin in the Sun* was filmed in 1961 and starred Sidney Poitier, Ruby Dee, and Claudia McNeil. (A 1989 version with Danny Glover and Esther Rolle gives a good sense of how the play lived on stage.) *Zoot Suit*, made in 1981 and starring Edward James Olmos, was filmed entirely in the theater where it was first performed. Watching any of these films will enhance the experience of reading the play.

9 Understanding Your Lines

One of the first things you will notice about a good play is the effectiveness of its language as an expression not only of meaning, but also of feeling and personality. Your study of your role, therefore, begins with respect for the details and implications of your character's language, which has been so carefully wrought by the author.

In everyday life, speech is the result of a process; you begin with a *germinal* idea or feeling, an impulse that needs to be formed into words. You then choose the words that will best communicate to others; although this *process of verbalization* usually happens almost instantaneously, complex thoughts and deep feelings sometimes require considerable effort to verbalize. A dramatic character on stage must go through this same process of verbalization, and you, the actor playing the character, must recreate and re-experience this process each and every time you speak your lines; it is the only way to keep your character's language alive, happening "right now, as if before our eyes." If you fail to relive this process of word choice, your lines will inevitably sound mechanical and rehearsed. As good actors say, you must come to "own" the character's words as if they were your own by recreating and re-experiencing the living process by which that language is formed. This requires working backward from the finished language provided by the writer to discover its genesis in the mind of the character.

In this step, you will explore the clues within the character's language that can lead you to a direct participation in the mind that produces that language.

Word Choice

The critical moment in the process of verbalization occurs when characters choose the words they speak in order to communicate an idea, feeling, or desire. This word choice is called *diction* (a word sometimes used to mean "enunciation," but here is used in its primary meaning, "choice of words to express ideas," as in "dictionary"). The words your character speaks have two kinds of meaning: their literal dictionary meanings, called *denotation*, and their implied emotional values, called *connotation*. We will consider denotation first.

Denotation is not a static thing; there may be several possible definitions for a word, and the meaning of words in popular usage sometimes changes quickly. You must be sure that the meaning you take for granted today is not a distortion of the playwright's original intention.

For example, Juliet, coming out on her balcony, says, "O Romeo. Romeo? Wherefore art thou Romeo?" Some young actresses deliver this line as if Juliet were wishing that Romeo were there, in the sense of "Romeo, where are you?" But when we discover that in Shakespeare's day *wherefore* meant "why," we see that she really is saying, "Why are you named Romeo, member of a family hated by my own?" Such obsolete meanings are sometimes labeled "archaic" in the dictionary.

Playwrights will sometimes manipulate denotation by *punning*, placing a word that has more than one denotation in a context where both meanings could be applied. Though puns have been called "the lowest form of humor," they may be used for both serious and comic effect. For example, when we examine the names of Beckett's characters in his play *Endgame*, we see that the name of the master "Hamm" reminds us of meat, while his servant "Clov" refers to the spice (clove) traditionally used with ham for flavor and preservation. But Beckett doesn't stop there; ham is meat that comes from an animal with a cloven hoof, and Clov does indeed act as the "feet" of Hamm, since Hamm cannot walk. There is also the "Ham actor," the tragedian, and Clov, the clown; and the overbearing Hamm (hammer) pounds down Clov (*clou* means "nail" in French) as well as the other two characters in the play, Nagg and Nell (*nagel* means "nail" in German). All these multiple meanings are wonderfully appropriate to the play.

Characters in plays frequently use topical and *colloquial* speech, the highly informal conversational language of a particular time and place. For example, calling a beautiful woman "a dish," "a real tomato," or her legs "a pair of gams," summons up 1930s America in a very specific way. Colloquial words and phrases tend to change meaning very quickly; doing a play only ten years old may require some investigation of the meaning of words and expressions it contains.

Good dictionaries will help you to be sure about denotation. For old plays, the *Oxford English Dictionary* (the "OED") lists the changing meanings of words with the dates of their currency. There are also carefully noted editions of great classical plays with glossaries and notes that are very helpful.

While denotation refers to the literal meaning of words, *connotation* is defined as "suggestive or associative implication of a term beyond its literal, explicit sense." The connotation of words can reveal the attitudes and feelings of a character. A dictionary will sometimes be helpful in giving examples of connotations, but the connotative possibilities of words are multiple and variable; the word *politic*, for example, is defined as "artful; ingenious; shrewd," but also "crafty; unscrupulous; cunning." You need to consider the *context* in order to determine which of the connotative possibilities of a word are appropriate. When Shakespeare's King Lear speaks of "a scurvy politician," we know just how he feels about the man. Likewise, when Blanche DuBois in *A Streetcar Named Desire* describes Stanley Kowalski as "swilling and gnawing and hulking," we understand not only her attitude toward Stanley, but also something about Blanche herself because she has chosen to express her disgust in such vividly bodily ways. The physical qualities of "swilling and gnawing and hulking" invite the actress to participate in the sensations they evoke, and this physicalization of the language can provide a strong sense not only of Blanche's disqust for Stanley, but also her barely suppressed sexuality.

To sum up, your understanding of your lines depends on your understanding of their meaning and feeling in an historical, social, and psychological context. You must consider *the meanings of the words when the play was written*, and *what feelings they express when used by this kind of character in this situation.*

One very good way to be sure you have examined the meanings of your lines is to *paraphrase* them, restate them in your own words, as if you were doing a translation of the original. Obviously, much of the emotional tone and poetic richness of the original will be lost, but you will have ensured that you have considered seriously the possible values of each word you speak.

EXERCISE 9.1: PARAPHRASE ON THREE LEVELS

Using one of the more important speeches from your scene, write a paraphrase of it on each of the following levels:

1. To express as simply as possible the *germinal idea* behind each sentence
2. To express the literal denotation, word by word
3. To express the connotations and emotional attitudes by pushing the feelings to an extreme using language that is natural to you

Try performing your paraphrase on each level.

Rhythm

The rhythm of speech refers to its tempo (fast or slow), its underlying "beat" (regular or irregular, heavy or light), and the variations of tempo and beat that provide *emphasis* on certain words or other elements of the speech and therefore contribute to meaning.

Rhythm is highly expressive of personality; the blustery, pompous person has a rhythm of speech much different from the thoughtful, introspective person. Even nationality and social background affect rhythm: the Irish, for example, tend to speak each thought on one long exhalation of breath, imparting an unmistakable rhythm to their speech. Good playwrights build the rhythms of speech that are appropriate to a character's personality and emotion, and your analysis of those rhythms will aid you in forming your characterization.

Many emotions have recognizable rhythmic implications. All emotion causes measurable changes in the tension of our muscles, and this tensing of the muscles has a direct effect on our speech. Take anger as an example: as anger rises in us, the body becomes tense, especially in the deep center where the largest muscles mobilize themselves for action. Tension in the interior muscles is communicated directly to the diaphragm, limiting its movement and forcing us to take shallow breaths, but since we need to oxygenate the muscles for defense purposes, we compensate by taking more rapid breaths. This causes us to break our speech up into shorter breath-phrases and to increase its tempo. Tension, spreading to the pharynx, causes an elevation of pitch, and coupled with the increased pressure of the breath stream, results in a "punching" delivery and increased volume. The tension moves into the jaw and encourages us to emphasize hard consonant sounds. As a result, our angry speech may become similar to the snapping and growling of an animal about to attack.

This very basic example shows you that both tone and rhythm are tied to your emotional state by the muscles that produce speech. A playwright or screenwriter knows that his or her dialogue will be performed aloud by actors, and so they write with a special sensitivity to the effect the words will have on the actor. By understanding the rhythms and tones your playwright has supplied for you, and by experiencing them in your own muscles as you pronounce them, you will have a chance to experience the feelings they express. An active physical participation in your character's language is a powerful tool for entering into the life of the character.

A skillful writer shapes rhythm on several levels at once. The fundamental rhythm is established by the flow of accented and unaccented syllables; we call this the *syllable cadence*. Look at the following example from Samuel Beckett's *Endgame*: you will see that Beckett has used rhythmic patterns of two and three syllables; read it aloud for full rhythmic effect; tap your feet.

> One day you'll be blind, like me. You'll be sitting there, a speck in the void, in the dark, forever, like me. (pause) One day you'll say to yourself, I'm tired. I'll sit down, and you'll go and sit down. Then you'll say, I'm hungry, I'll get up and get something to eat. But you won't get up. You'll say, I shouldn't have sat down, but since I have I'll sit on a little longer, then I'll get up and get something to eat. (pause) But you won't get up and you won't get anything to eat. (pause) And there you'll be, like a little bit of grit, in the middle of the steppe.

The rhythmic flow of these syllables is as highly developed as any formal poetry.

The next level of rhythm is the *breath cadence*, and this is of special importance to the actor. The evolution of our written language was greatly influenced by the physical act of speaking, and we tend to divide our thoughts into sentences that can be said in one breath; when the thought is complex enough to require several phrases, we separate these into "sub-breaths" by commas, semicolons, or colons (in music, the comma is still used as a breath mark). Playwrights manipulate breath cadences to guide the actor into a pattern of breathing, and the rhythm of breath is a primary factor in emotion. Try reading the Beckett piece aloud with a small breath at every comma, a full breath at each period, and a large breath at each "(pause)." What emotional experience results? Next, try the same experiment using the speech you paraphrased in Exercise 9.1.

Finally, the dialogue itself as the characters speak in turn has a rhythm. Each speech usually contains a central idea and functions in a way similar to paragraphs in prose, and the alternation of the speeches creates the *dialogue cadence*. We get a good impression of the tempo of a scene by looking at the density of the printed script; a mass of long speeches suggests a different approach to tempo than, for example, the extremely short back-and-forth exchange of some comedy.

Here is a summary of these cadences or levels of rhythm:

1. syllabic cadence
2. breath cadence
3. dialogue cadence

Remember that the rhythm of speech does not absolutely determine meaning or even emotion; your choices must be based upon your understanding of the meaning of the line, taking into account the demands of character and situation. Nevertheless, by recognizing the rhythms and sounds the writer has built into your character's speech, and by experiencing them fully in your own muscles, you will find them a powerful aid in entering into the consciousness of your character. As Stanislavski said:

> There is an indissoluble interdependence, interaction and bond between tempo-rhythm and feeling. . . . The correctly established tempo-rhythm of a play or a role, can of itself, intuitively (on occasion automatically) take hold of the feelings of an actor and arouse in him a true sense of living his part.[1]

Melody

There is a story about the famous Italian actress Eleanora Duse. Her speech, it was said, was so emotionally rich that she once moved a New York audience to tears by reading from the Manhattan telephone book. True or not, the story shows that any good actor develops great expressiveness in the use of the sounds of speech, and playwrights are careful to provide language that is rich in its tonal potential, whatever quality it may have, from the lyrical sweep of Tennessee Williams to the curt staccato of David Mamet.

There have been attempts to develop systems that attach certain meanings to certain sounds. The most famous of these was the *Roback Voco-Sensory Theory*. In one of his experiments, subjects were asked to tell which three-letter nonsense syllable, "mil" or "mal," made them think of larger or smaller objects. As you might guess, most subjects thought that "mal" meant something bigger than "mil." The theory

---

[1]From Constantin Stanislavski, *Building a Character*, trans. Elizabeth Reynolds Hapgood (New York: Theatre Arts Books, 1949), pp. 218–236. Theatre Arts Books, 153 Waverly Place, New York, NY 10014.

points out that the physical act of saying "mal" requires opening the mouth more than does saying "mil," and this causes the sensation of bigness associated with "mal." The opposite is true for "mil," which is a "smaller" sound. The theory goes on to suggest that much of language was formed by this sort of translation of the physical sensations of speaking: "rough" words *feel* rough, and smooth words *feel* smooth, for example, just as *rushing* rushes, *explodes* explodes, and so on.

This theory has great limitations, however, since many words do not seem to relate to their physical qualities; for instance, "small" is made up of big sounds, while "big" is small. Nevertheless, the theory provides an interesting view of language for the actor since it encourages a way of speaking that emphasizes the relationship of physical sensation and the meaning and feeling of speech. Try reading the previous speech from Samuel Beckett's *Endgame* so as to emphasize its tonal values. Feel how Beckett has selected words whose sounds can be useful to you in supporting the meaning and emotional tone of the speech. Feel especially the shift from "big" open vowel sounds in the main body of the speech to the "little" hard consonant sounds in the last line; do you see how this shift can communicate a vivid experience of the isolation and insignificance the speaker feels?

Stanislavski, in *Building a Character*, sums it up this way:

> Letters, syllables, words—these are the musical notes of speech, out of which we fashion measures, arias, whole symphonies. There is good reason to describe beautiful speech as musical. . . . Musical speech opens up endless possibilities of conveying the inner life of a role.[2]

Tone and rhythm give our speech color and individual flavor, and make it fully human. Through careful and informed analysis of your lines, you can unlock these inherent values of tone and rhythm, and by surrendering yourself to the muscular actions required to produce them, you can bring them back to life for your audience.

EXERCISE 9.2: RHYTHM AND MELODY POLARIZATION

Using the same speech you chose for your paraphrase (Exercise 9.1), analyze its rhythmic and tonal qualities. Use markings, colored pencils, or other devices to help recognize the rhythmic and tonal patterns in the speech.

1. Using large bodily movements and nonverbal sound, create a "musical dance" of the speech that exaggerates its rhythmic and tonal patterns. Move from your deep center, involve your breath.
2. Then immediately do the speech as written, but this time speak the words without moving. See how much of your body's memory of the first version carries over to enrich the speech as your deep muscles continue to respond to it even without external movement.

---

[2]From Constantin Stanislavski, *Building a Character*, trans. Elizabeth Reynolds Hapgood (New York: Theatre Arts Books, 1949), pp. 218-236. Theatre Arts Books, 153 Waverly Place, New York, NY 10014.

3. With your partner, examine your scene as a whole. Does the dialogue cadence give you any clues about the way the scene should flow? Create a "musical dance" of the entire scene between you, throwing a ball back and forth as the dialogue flows.

Summary of Step 9

When you set out to create a role, you necessarily begin with the character's language. You must come to "own" these words as if they were your own by recreating and re-experiencing the living process by which that language is formed. This requires working backward from the finished language provided by the writer to discover its genesis in the mind of the character.

The words your character speaks have two kinds of meaning: their dictionary meanings, called *denotation*, and their emotional values, called *connotation*. While denotation refers to the literal meaning of words, *connotation* can reveal the attitudes and feelings of a character. You must consider *the meanings of the words when the play was written*, and *what feelings they express when used by this kind of character in this situation*. One way to be sure you have examined the meanings of your lines is to *paraphrase* them, to restate them in your own words.

Good playwrights build the rhythms and tonality of speech that are appropriate to a character's personality and emotion. The character's language is tied to your emotional state by the muscles that produce speech; an active physical participation in your character's language is a powerful tool for entering into the character's mind.

STEP

10 Understanding Play and Scene Structure

You will continue your introduction to script analysis by understanding how plays and film scripts are shaped for maximum dramatic effect. To do this, you will first explore the underlying principles of the shape and necessary qualities of drama through a simple exercise.

EXERCISE 10.1: A DRAMATIC BREATH

1. Take a single, complete breath that is as *dramatic* as you can make it. Don't think about it, just do it!
2. Consider the things you did to make the breath more dramatic. If you are in a group situation, discuss it and see if there was something that everyone did.

When trying this exercise for the first time, most people exaggerate their breath, making it louder; they may also add movement to the breath to make it more visible. Some people take a faster or slower breath than normal. These things, however, are limited to the external aspects of the breath; they serve to make the breath more theatrical, not necessarily more *dramatic*. Do you understand the difference? The sense of drama is deeper than such external considerations; it implies an experience that involves us in a more fundamental way, and can take many different external forms.

Consider for a moment those situations in real life that are naturally dramatic. Let's use a sporting event as an example: what are the things that make for a really dramatic football, baseball, or basketball game?

For one thing, games between teams that are evenly matched, especially when they are longtime rivals, can be special fun because the sense of conflict is greater. *Conflict* literally means "to strike together," so any situation in which two forces are opposed creates a sense of drama. It can exist even within a single person: when you hold your breath, for example, there is a conflict between your determination to hold your breath and your need to release it; in a sense, your mind is at war with your body. Most plays and film scripts are driven by a central conflict. For example, in *The Glass Menagerie*, the central conflict is within Tom—a conflict between independence and responsibility. Tom needs to leave home to find his own identity, but he feels an obligation to stay to help his sister

64

and mother. This conflict is universal because all children feel something like it when it is time for them to leave the nest, even if their parents and siblings are not as needy as Laura and Amanda.

Games can be more dramatic when they are more *significant*. Perhaps the championship is at stake, or the teams are long-standing rivals. The stakes are raised, and the higher the stakes, the greater the drama can be. In the exercise, some of you may have increased the "importance" of your breath by taking a deeper breath. This deeper breath contained more energy and was therefore more significant than normal. Notice, however, that a significant breath may not necessarily be bigger or louder; the significance of the breath depends not on these external qualities but on its inner *dynamic*, the amount of energy it contains. For example, imagine a situation in which you are hiding from a killer in a dark, silent room; your life depends on making no noise or movement. How would you breathe? Can you feel that your breathing is highly significant and dramatic even though it is invisible and inaudible? Just so, the conflict underlying *The Glass Menagerie* is crucial to Tom's sense of himself; it is, in a psychological sense, a matter of life and death, but it is expressed through small actions.

Perhaps more than any other single quality, the drama of a game depends on the outcome being in doubt. The closer the score, the greater the drama can be; if one team gets too far ahead, we lose interest. Think back to the exercise: how might you put the outcome of your breath in doubt? The best way would be to hold it. While you are holding it, we wonder "When will he or she breathe out?" This is suspense in its purest form: *an aroused energy that wants to be released but is literally "held up."* The most important question in the theater is, "What will happen?"

If the suspense of a game can last to the very last play, the drama is tremendous. Just so, the longer you hold your breath, the more the suspense *builds* toward a climax. This is a common strategy in plays, where the outcome is held in doubt as long as possible, thereby raising the level of suspense higher and higher. We call this rise and fall of the energy the *arc* of the play, and the greater the arc, the greater the drama. You may have increased the arc of your breath by building to a high point then releasing it more deeply. We enjoy this sense of release, which in drama is called *climax*.

To sum up, then, our definition of a dramatic event is *a conflict in which the stakes are high and the outcome is in doubt and builds toward a climax.*

EXERCISE 10.2: THE DRAMA OF THE PLAY

Consider the play from which your scene comes. What makes it dramatic?

1. What is the basic conflict?
2. What makes this conflict significant? What is at stake?
3. What is the source of suspense? How is the outcome kept in doubt?
4. What is the climax?

Finding the Crisis

In a well-constructed play, the sequence of events (the *plot*) moves forward as suspense builds; we begin to wonder "How will this come out?" When the conflict is just on the verge of being resolved, suspense is at its peak. This moment of greatest suspense, as the outcome hangs in the balance, is called a *crisis* (a "turning point"). The function of everything that happens before the crisis is to lead toward it with *rising* energy, while everything after the crisis flows naturally from it with a *falling* sense of resolution. Recall the single breath you took in Exercise 10.1. As you inhaled, the dynamic energy rose; when you began to hold the breath, the period of crisis began; the longer you held it, the more the suspense built; the exact moment when you decided to exhale ended the crisis; and the exhaling itself was the climax of the breath.

This is how most plays are shaped. For example, in *The Glass Menagerie*, the idea of finding a gentleman caller who could marry Laura and thereby release Tom from his family obligations is established early, in the second scene of the play. The main body of the play works out the details of the plan, and suspense mounts as Tom actually manages to bring Jim home. Suspense peaks as Jim dances with Laura and we sense that perhaps the plan might actually succeed; the crisis is finally reached when Jim tells Laura that he is in love with someone else:

> **LAURA** *[FAINTLY]*:   You—won't—call again?
>
> **JIM:**   No, Laura, I can't.

The climax flows quickly from this; Laura falls back even more deeply into her dependency, and Tom leaves home just minutes later, wracked by guilt.

This, then, is the fundamental shape of all dramatic events: a rising conflict, a crisis, and a resolution (see Figure 10.1). It is a shape common to all of the performing arts—symphonies and ballets have it. It is the fundamental unit of rhythm, because it is the shape of a muscular contraction and relaxation. It is the fundamental shape of life itself, from birth to death. It lives within a single breath or even a single step.

EXERCISE 10.3: A DRAMATIC STEP

1. Try taking a single step as dramatically as you can. Again, just do it without thinking about it.
2. Consider what you did; did you feel the *crisis* of the step?
3. Try it again, and this time let your breath parallel your step: feel the rising energy as you step forward and inhale; prolong the crisis by holding the breath as you begin to shift your weight from your back foot to your front; feel the exact moment when the crisis passes as your weight shifts; then enjoy a full climax as you finish the step and exhale.

In this exercise you experienced how finding the crisis of the step helped to unify and clarify the flow of the action of the step. Just so, you can understand the

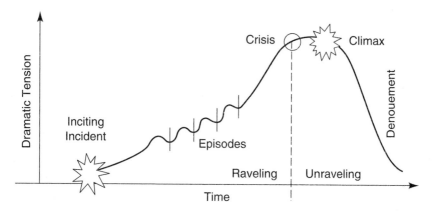

FIGURE 10.1   The Shape of Drama.

shape of an entire play by identifying its crisis. Having recognized the crisis, you can then feel how everything before it flows up to it, and how everything there-after flows from it. One way to define the crisis of a play is "that moment after which the outcome of the play is inevitable" or "the last moment at which the play might have a different ending."

EXERCISE 10.4: FINDING THE CRISIS

Working with your scene partner, discuss your play. Think backward from the end: what is the crisis? Is the crisis prolonged over a period of time? Can you identify the exact moment when the turning point is reached and the climax becomes inevitable?

Units of Action

A play is made up of many parts, each of which advances the action toward the crisis and climax. Plays may be divided into acts, and the acts into scenes; actors understand that scenes may themselves be divided into smaller units of action called "beats." We will explore this important idea in greater detail in Step 15, but for now you will explore how individual small units of action can connect to form larger patterns. This is an idea more easily understood by the muscles than the mind, so let's try a physical exercise to experience units of action.

EXERCISE 10.5: UNITS OF ACTION

Perform each of the following actions and experience the dramatic potential of each. Remember to focus on the crisis in each pattern: treat all that goes before as leading up to the crisis and all that follows as flowing from it.

1. Again, experience the dramatic shape of a single step. Experiment with differ-ently shaped steps: a long rise, a long crisis, and a quick release; then a short rise, a short crisis, and a long release; and so on.

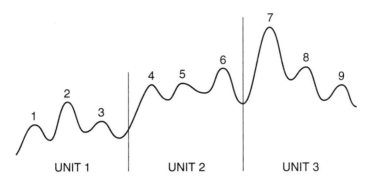

FIGURE 10.2   Compound Action. Here, nine steps divided into three units go together to produce one larger pattern.

2. Take three steps experienced as one phrase, with the crisis in the third step. The first two steps have mini-crises of their own, but now they lead up to the main crisis of the unit of three in the third step. Let your breath parallel the pattern of your steps.
3. Now try nine steps divided into three units of three steps each, with the crisis of this larger pattern in the last group (as in Figure 10.2). Try it again with the crisis in the first group of steps.
4. Invent patterns of your own; add sound.

In this exercise you experienced how small units of action can form a larger pattern of action having a shape of its own. Likewise, these larger phrases can be connected into still larger patterns, which again have shapes of their own. On all these levels, the fundamental shape of rise, crisis, and release is the same, even though the proportion of the parts may be different (see Figure 10.2).

This is how the parts of a play or screenplay go together to make the whole. The "smallest" units of action, the individual *interactions* between characters, work together to form the units of action we call *beats*, each of which has a crisis of its own; the beats work together to form a *scene* which has a crisis of its own; finally, the scenes flow together to lead us to the *main crisis* of the entire story.

Finding the Function and Crisis of the Scene

Rehearsing a scene is much like making a map of an unknown territory. You and your partners, through trial and error, must discover for yourselves the pathway of the scene's energy, the logic of its flow of cause and effect hidden beneath the surface of the dialogue.

You can best begin by understanding the dramatic purpose of the scene within the story as a whole: ask yourselves, "What happens in this scene that changes the world of the play? Why couldn't this scene be cut from the story?" Understanding the scene's purpose can help to guide your rehearsal exploration and establish priorities that will make your work more efficient.

Next you begin to explore the pathway through which the scene's energy flows, interaction by interaction, and the shape that the writer has given to this flow. Your work so far has helped you to understand that the energy of the scene will flow up toward the *scene crisis*, then flow away from it. The crisis of the scene is the major milestone on the journey you and your partner are discovering. It takes some time in rehearsal to find it, but your exploration will be more efficient if you agree on it in a general way as you set out.

The crisis can be identified by thinking backward from the end of the scene, looking for the moment in which the outcome of the scene most hangs in the balance, the moment when the outcome of the scene is determined. Ask yourselves: given the way the scene comes out, what is the last moment when it might turn out differently? (This same strategy of "reading backward" also works for finding the crisis of the play as a whole.)

You will notice that moments of crisis are almost always choices made by one of the characters, and so they usually occur "between the lines." You will also notice that scenes do not usually have a strong sense of resolution or climax after the crisis, since they must move the story forward by leading us on into the next scene.

Though you may analyze the scene's structure by breaking it down intellectually in this way at first, experienced actors usually approach structure intuitively, developing a shared rhythmic experience of the rise and fall of the scene's energy as they explore it in rehearsal. However you find it, your sense of scene structure must finally live as a sort of underlying "dance" as you and your partners feel the energy of the scene moving and building toward the crisis, then flowing naturally from it.

EXERCISE 10.6: FINDING AND EXPERIENCING THE CRISIS OF THE SCENE (FIRST READ-THROUGH)

Working with your partner, answer these questions about your scene:

1. What is the major change in the world of the play that occurs in this scene? How does this scene cause the plot to progress? How does it enhance the meaning of the play?
2. What is the crisis of the scene, the moment when the outcome is determined?
3. How does this scene grow out of the scene before, and lead into the scene to follow?

Now read through the scene aloud. Feel how the action of the scene flows up toward the crisis, then flows from it.

Summary of Step 10

A dramatic event has *a conflict in which the stakes are high and the outcome is in doubt and builds toward a climax.* The moment when the outcome hangs in the balance is called the *crisis* ("turning point"). Everything before the crisis leads toward it with *rising* energy, and everything after it flows from it with *falling* energy. The fundamental shape of rise, crisis, and release is the same on each of the several levels on which action operates: the individual *interactions* between characters work together to form the units of action we call *beats*, each of which has a mini-crisis; the beats work together to form a *scene* which has a crisis of its own; finally, the scenes flow together to lead us to the *main crisis* of the entire story. As you begin to rehearse a scene, it will be useful to understand the function of the scene within the overall story, and to identify the moment of crisis within the scene. You then begin to work together to find the "dance" of the scene as the action flows up to the crisis, then away from it toward the next scene.

11 Experiencing the Character's Function and Given Circumstances

Now that you understand the function and structure of your scene, you will turn your attention to your character and his or her given circumstances. As we discussed in Part One, your character was created to do a specific job within the scheme of the play as a whole. We call this the *dramatic function* of the character and understanding this function will inspire and guide your work in rehearsal. One note of caution, however. You are not interested in constructing a blueprint or outline for the character in advance, and then simply filling it in. Rather, you search continuously throughout the rehearsal process to discover and meet the needs for which the character was created. A full understanding of dramatic function will develop only gradually as you work.

This is important because too often actors approach their characters so personally that they begin to forget the larger purpose for which that character was created. Without an ongoing sense of purpose, you may create a character who is alive and believable, but who doesn't do the job it was created to do within the story as a whole. The audience may be impressed by such a performance, but the story will suffer and you will have failed in your main responsibility. As Stanislavski put it, the actor's most important task is *to understand how every moment of the performance and every aspect of characterization contributes to the reason the play was written.*

For example, in *Death of a Salesman*, Willy Loman is a man who, like many of his generation, measures his value as a human being by his success in his work. Such people suffer terribly when they lose their jobs, or even when they retire, because they don't know themselves without their work. When Willy loses his job, he feels worthless; he no longer feels worthy even of the love of his family. Eventually, he makes the only "sale" he has left—his suicide which enables his family to collect on his life insurance. We can say, then, that Willy's dramatic function is to represent the many people who are encouraged by our highly materialistic and competitive society to think that earning money and approval is the only source of self-esteem. Such people, like Willy, confuse *material* and *spiritual* values, and this, Miller is saying, can be a tragic misunderstanding of the American Dream. Sadly, in our age of corporate downsizing, when entire professions are being made obsolete by technology, we see many people in Willy Loman's situation.

A Raisin in the Sun is also a play about the American Dream. The title of the play refers to a poem by Langston Hughes in which unfulfilled dreams shrivel up "like a raisin in the sun." Every member of the Younger family has a dream, and Walter, like Willy Loman, wants to win self-esteem by making money. As he tells his wife, "I got to take hold of this here world, baby!" His scheme to open a liquor store is driven by his sense of failure: all he has to give his son "is stories about how rich white people live . . . . " He is so driven that, like Willy Loman, he makes misguided choices. By the end of the play, however, it is Mama's dream of a home of their own that prevails because it will unite the family; they will risk fighting racial discrimination because they believe they can succeed if they stick together.

In its own way, *Zoot Suit* also examines the American Dream. Henry Reyna, and his alter ego El Pachuco, search for dignity, justice, and self-identity within a culture that deprives them of all three. They face a choice similar to that facing the Younger family in *A Raisin in the Sun:* how best to live authentically and combat the forces of discrimination? Some of the characters in *Zoot Suit* urge defiance and even violence; some urge assimilation into the white culture; some urge a retreat into the family and ethnic tradition. The ultimate choice is not as important, Valdez would say, as confronting the discrimination that makes such a choice necessary.

In *The Glass Menagerie*, Tom longs for the freedom to pursue his own life and thereby to discover his own identity. He is held back by his sense of obligation to his family, especially to his disabled sister. He is "the man of the house" and fears that if he leaves, it will be very hard for Amanda and Laura to get by. His only hope, then, is to find a replacement "man of the house" for Laura; Jim the gentleman caller is that hope, and it is a bitter irony that Jim fails to fulfill that hope because he is himself consumed by another example of the American Dream, a dream of power and wealth.

In each play, every member of the cast must understand the tone and meaning of the whole (what Stanislavski called "the reason why the play was written") and how his or her character contributes to that tone and meaning. There are two main ways that characters may serve the story: by advancing the plot through their actions, and by contributing to the meaning of the play through the values which they and their actions express. In terms of the *plot*, your character may do things which drive the plot forward, may be a "foil" to frustrate the objectives of another character, or may simply provide some information essential to the story. In terms of the *meaning* of the story, your character may represent certain values or present a contrast to the values of other characters, may be the spokesperson for one of several conflicting points of view, or, as we have seen, may be an embodiment of some quality or some aspect of the conflict within the main character.

EXERCISE 11.1: DRAMATIC FUNCTION (SECOND READ-THROUGH)

After reading the entire play or script from which your scene comes, work with your partner to determine the dramatic function of your characters. Answer these questions:

1. If your character were to be eliminated from the story, what would be missing from the plot?
2. How would the meaning of the play suffer if your character were cut? Is there some value or point of view expressed by your character? Does your character contribute to an understanding of other characters?

With your partner, again read the scene aloud to the group. Discuss your understanding of the dramatic functions of your characters.

Function and Recognition Traits

The writer has given your character certain traits that make his or her actions seem "natural" to them. These are called *function* traits because they permit the character to believably fulfill his or her dramatic function within the story.

Willy Loman, for example, is a man who sells. Eventually, we realize that he is selling himself. He feels that he is worthless until he persuades others, even his own sons, of his value. Though Willy has many other traits, it is this deep *insecurity* that allows him to fulfill his main function believably. Whatever else an actor may do in his portrayal of Willy, he must embody this function trait first and foremost and let no other trait obscure or confuse it.

Similarly, Walter in *A Raisin in the Sun* is desperate *to feel like a worthy father*, Beneatha wants *to find and fulfill her own identity* by serving the world meaningfully, and Mama wants *to bind her family together*. Henry in *Zoot Suit* wants *to be treated with dignity* and respect and is prone to self-destructive rage when he isn't treated this way, Della is torn between her unconditional love of Henry and her own dignity, and Alice is driven more by a passion for social justice than by love for Henry. Tom in *The Glass Menagerie* feels trapped by his family obligation; Laura feels crippled in both body and soul, even though her bad leg may not be as great a deformity as she feels it to be; and Amanda, despite her protestations to the contrary, unconsciously encourages the dependency of her children as a way of bolstering her own sense of worthiness.

It is not surprising that at a deep level, all of these characters are driven by fundamental human needs like the desire for self-esteem, love, or security. Drama, after all, portrays universal patterns of human experience that we can all recognize and share.

This quality of *recognition*, then, is important in a characterization. As Aristotle said in *The Poetics*, we must be able to recognize characters as fellow human beings, *even if we do not like them*. A performance must therefore include traits which "round out" the character and make us recognize him or her as a real and specific human being who is in some way "like" us or people we know or know about: we call these *recognition* traits.

Although some recognition traits have been provided by the writer, this is an area in which the actor may contribute personal touches to the role that makes it his or her "own." Arthur Miller tells us, for example, that Willy's wife loves him in spite of "his mercurial nature, his temper, his massive dreams and little cruelties." Willy probably tries hard to be fun with his male friends and is probably a bit of a flirt with the women. His mercurial nature makes him quick to anger but just as quick to be remorseful and apologetic. His great pride may sometimes drive him to be cruelly demeaning to others, as in his contempt for Charley's son. All these traits help to round him out as a recognizable human being.

Recognition traits can also be physical and vocal: Willy might be a bit of a dandy in the way he dresses and carries himself in scenes from his earlier life, but he might be so disheartened later in life that he has let himself go both in body and dress; when Dustin Hoffman played him, Willy had even developed a quivering hand and lip. There are many such recognition traits an actor might give Willy, some of which might be surprising or even contradictory to one another—people, after all, are complex. Whatever such traits the actor may contribute out of his own personality and imagination, none of them must be allowed to obscure Willy's main function trait of profound insecurity.

Remember that these early analytical ideas are meant only to help you understand the essence of the character; you may well eventually discover your own way of expressing that essence.

You learn all you can about the character from the evidence within the text itself. You consider the character's age, physical traits, the kind of culture and historical period he or she comes from, his or her social and economic class, educational background, and the nature of the character's family life. If this information is not supplied by the text, it may be useful for you to invent some of it for yourself, though you must be careful to do this in a manner that supports and extends the character's function and qualities as determined by the author.

Remember that all this basic information about the character is intended only to inspire and guide your exploration in rehearsal; you must not simply "put it on" as if it were a mask or costume. You will have to discover your own way of playing this role and you may ultimately discover for yourself new forms of appearance and behavior within the parameters established by the writer and with respect for the character's dramatic function.

EXERCISE 11.2: FUNCTION AND RECOGNITION TRAITS

Examine your character in the scene again.

1. What traits must the character have in order to believably perform his or her function within the play, such as insecurity, ambition, vengefulness, or irresponsibility? How has the playwright provided or implied these traits?

2. What additional traits has the playwright provided or implied which help to round out your character as a recognizable human being, such as a sense of humor, particular quirks, or superstitions?

The Given Circumstances

Psychologists say that personality is shaped both by "nature" and "nurture." Think of the ways your own personality has been shaped both by your genetic inheritance (your nature) and by the world in which you grew up (your nurture). Every day, you interact with your world. It has physical, psychological, and social aspects that profoundly influence your feelings and thoughts. In reaction to these experiences, your personality is continuing to change and evolve in the direction established by your nature.

A character in a play or film has been given a nature by the author, and the author may even tell us something of the character's personal background prior to the beginning of the play. But the character is also shaped by nurture, by his or her interaction with the world created by the author, a world created specifically to serve the story and the character. As an actor, then, you must work not only on the inner qualities of your character, but also strive to experience the character's world and let your characterization develop within it.

The specific qualities of the character's world are called the *given circumstances*. These "givens" fall into three categories: *who*, *where*, and *when*. Let's briefly examine each.

Who

Because personality is formed and influenced by our interactions with those around us, your character can be fully understood only by examining the *relationship* between him or her and all the other characters, whether they are physically present in your scene or not. These relationships have two aspects: the *general* and the *specific*. The general relationship provides basic considerations that make a relationship similar to others of its kind, whereas the specific relationship reveals what is unique to this particular case.

For example, in *Death of a Salesman*, Willy has a *general* relationship with his neighbor Charley. Like many neighbors, they talk about their work and their families and even give each other advice. But Willy and Charley also have a *specific* relationship that is very important to the overall meaning of the play. Charley is an easygoing man who, unlike Willy, has strong self-esteem. Charley advises Willy to accept himself and his life and be thankful for all he has. He even offers Willy a job, one that Willy's pride will not allow him to accept. In all, Charley represents a worldview that, if Willy could adopt it, might save his life.

Charley is sharply contrasted by Willy's brother Ben, who lives like a ghost in Willy's mind. Ben is the ultimate embodiment of the American Dream. Like the popular folk hero Horatio Alger, he tells Willy to "go West" and seek his fortune. One of the most important scenes in the play occurs when Willy is playing cards with Charley while at the same time talking to the image of Ben. This scene shows us Willy being torn between the two ways of life embodied by Charley and Ben, neither of which he can really accept because of his deep-seated insecurity. At the end of the play, we see the contrast of Charley and Ben carried on by Willy's sons. Happy declares, "He had a good dream. It's the only dream you can have—to come out number-one man." But Biff says only, "I know who I am, kid." All of these characters can be fully understood within their general and specific relationships.

Where

Where the play happens has two main aspects: the *physical* and the *social*. The *physical* environment has a tremendous influence on the action. For example, Shakespeare chose to set a play of great passion, *Othello*, in the hot and humid climate of Cyprus, whereas his play of intrigue and indecision, *Hamlet*, is properly set in the cold and isolated climate of Denmark. Likewise, the urban setting and the terribly cramped quarters of the apartments in *A Raisin in the Sun* and *The Glass Menagerie* embody Walter's and Tom's feelings of being trapped in a life over which they have no control.

The *social* environment is also of great importance. We've already mentioned the importance of the American Dream in these plays; the values of the working class are fundamental in them. The hysteria over World War II in *Zoot Suit* gives free rein to the innate prejudice against Mexican Americans, and the prideful culture of the Pachucos serves to inflame the confrontation. Likewise, the social climate of the bar in which *Cheers* is set is very much a character in the show. It is a home away from home, a place "where everybody knows your name." Here the characters share their most intimate feelings and problems, as Diane and Carla do in our sample scene (see Appendix A). In this scene, the spunky, street-tough, lower-class Carla freely shares her feelings with her coworker, the classy, beautiful, but neurotic, Diane. Carla's boyfriend, Ben Ludlow, is an eminent psychotherapist who is attracted to Carla because she is the only one in the bar who *doesn't* treat him with reverence. As in any good dramatic writing, each of the characters in *Cheers* was developed in relationship to all the others. Diane, for example, is the outsider who is a "fish out of water" in the world of *Cheers*, but she and the denizens of the bar gradually learn to relate to one another despite their great differences. In our sample scene, we see her even giving heartfelt advice to the tough Carla.

Minor characters, like Ben Ludlow in our sample scene, and Bobo in *A Raisin in the Sun*, are usually given virtually no history and limited delineation.

We might know only that one is an eminent psychologist, another a small, frightened, unsuccessful businessman. It is up to the actor to flesh these characters out in a way that is interesting, believable, and appropriate to their function, but with a sense of economy that reflects their importance within the story.

When

When a scene is happening is important in terms of the *time of day* and *season*. *Death of a Salesman* begins in the summer, the season of warmth, growth, and fulfillment, and ends in the fall, the season of cold, decay, and impending death.

The *historical period* of a play, with all its implications of manners, values, and beliefs, is another important aspect of the "when." Most of *The Glass Menagerie* is a memory of the 1930s, before World War II, and Tom tells us in his first speech that the Great Depression and "labor disturbances" at home and civil unrest overseas are "the social background of the play." We have already mentioned the importance of World War II to *Zoot Suit*. *A Raisin in the Sun* is set in the years after World War II when many African American men returned from the war and an integrated army only to find that racism still oppressed them at home. *Cheers* is set in the present, but the bar has a timeless quality. It is a refuge from the real world, and so the producers were careful to avoid many of the issues and current news events that other television shows often use for plot material.

Here is a list of the givens:

1. Who
   a. General relationship
   b. Specific relationship
2. Where
   a. Physical environment
   b. Social environment
3. When
   a. Time of day
   b. Season
   c. Historical period

Each of these given circumstances must be evaluated as to its relative importance; don't waste thought and energy on aspects of the character's world that do not contribute to the action and meaning of the play.

If the givens of the play are foreign to you, some research will be required. In period plays, the history, architecture, painting, music, religion, politics, and fashion of the time can be very useful. Even contemporary plays may involve circumstances and language that are unfamiliar to you.

When possible, actually experiencing the most important givens can be a great help in rehearsing a scene. Consider working in locations that approximate the conditions of the scene. For example, I have several times held rehearsals for Shakespeare's *A Midsummer Night's Dream* in the woods at night by lantern light, because the "sense memory" of this experience greatly enriches the stage performance. In the same spirit, a director friend once forbid anyone in his cast to speak to the actor playing an alienated character, even outside of rehearsals.

A note of caution: beginning actors sometimes try to "indicate" the givens. Remember: it is not your job to *show* the audience anything about the character's world. Your job is simply to *live* in that world and let it affect you.

EXERCISE 11.3: THE GIVENS (THIRD READ-THROUGH)

1. Working with your partner, analyze the given circumstances of your scene and discuss the influence of each on your character and on the action.
2. Rehearse the scene in ways that help you to experience the influence of the givens. For example, you might rehearse in a place that provides similar conditions as the world of the play.
3. Read your scene for the group. Try to experience the givens as fully as possible.
4. Afterward, discuss with the group the sense of the givens they got from your reading and the influence of the givens on the scene.

Summary of Step 11

Your character was created to do a specific job within the play; we called this his or her *dramatic function*. Every aspect of your performance must contribute to this function. There are two main ways your character may serve the story: by advancing the *plot*, and by contributing to the *meaning* of the play. Your character has been given certain *function* traits so he or she can believably fulfill his or her purpose within the story. A performance must also include traits which round out the character and make us recognize him or her as a real and specific human being; we call these *recognition* traits.

The character was created in relationship to other characters and within a particular world. These *given circumstances* (*who*, *where*, and *when*) are essential to a proper understanding and experience of the character.

Summary of Part Three

Your brief analysis of the script has given you a basic understanding of the most important aspects of your role and the scene: you understand the function of your character within the plot and meaning of the play; you have experienced how your scene fits into the structure of the whole play and how the scene itself is shaped around a crisis; and you have experienced how the given circumstances of who, where, and when affect the action and the character. You will now put this information to work as you and your partner explore the living experience of the scene in rehearsal.

PART FOUR

Rehearsal

At last the real work begins. The information you have gathered through analysis can make your rehearsal exploration more efficient and fruitful, but it is only a preparation for the actual work of rehearsal, not a substitute for it. The true life of the character will be found only by working with your fellow actors and director through trial and error and the accumulation of experience in rehearsal.

Let's look at this process. First, you will put yourself into the character's world, his or her *given circumstances*, and experience them for yourself. In the character's circumstances, you begin to experience the character's *needs* for yourself, perhaps recognizing similar needs from your own life. You then begin to experience the *objectives* the character chooses in hope of satisfying those needs. These objectives motivate you to say and do the things the character says and does—his or her *actions*. As you begin to experience your character's world, needs, choices, objectives, and actions, you will find that emotion and the character's personality will begin to form in you, naturally and automatically.

This is the process of transformation that Stanislavski called *metamorphosis*. Just as your real-life personality has been formed and continues to evolve as you interact with your world, so the character will grow during rehearsals as a new "me," a new version of your "I," forms under the influence of your experience of your character's circumstances, needs, objectives, actions, interactions, and relationships. As your acting skills develop, you may be able to work more efficiently and effectively, but there are no shortcuts. No amount of posturing, false voice, or trumped-up emotion can substitute for this natural process of transformation.

Getting and Giving Notes

Throughout the rehearsal process, you will depend on the feedback you get about your work from others. Actors depend on feedback more than most other artists; the notes you get from your teachers, directors, and fellow actors are tremendously important in guiding the development of your role and your growth as an artist. Therefore actors have a solemn responsibility to provide accurate and useful feedback to one another. Many of the following exercises require you to discuss your work and the work of others. Use these principles for effective communication:

1. Don't guess what is going on inside someone else; instead, say what you *see* and how it makes you *feel*. Don't say, "Why are you hiding?" Say, "I noticed that you rarely looked at your partner during this scene, and that made me feel as if you were hiding."
2. Take the time to be *clear* about your message before you deliver it.
3. Be *specific*, *simple*, and *direct*.
4. Above all, remember that our aim is to support and respect one another and the work itself. Keep your focus on the work and off of personalities.

12 Personalizing

Like your own behavior in everyday life, your character's behavior is driven by needs. When you feel a need, you are energized—you feel that you have to *do* something, even if you don't know immediately what it is. This arousal can be either positive, as in the anticipation of something pleasurable, or negative, as in the fear of something painful.

As in life, characters may postpone acting on their needs because of external or internal obstacles. You know from your own experience that the longer an important need is suppressed, the stronger it becomes. This fact helps writers to build suspense in a play or film. Shakespeare's Hamlet, for example, spends a great deal of time wondering whether to avenge his father's murder; he finds one excuse after another for not acting on his need. We begin to wonder, how much longer will he wait? What will happen? The tension becomes greater and greater with each passing scene. In the last scene of the play, circumstance will not permit him to delay any longer, and his action finally explodes.

Hamlet, however, is an unusual character. Most characters, like most people, act on their needs soon after they are felt. Usually, the sequence of events develops like this: something happens that arouses a need in you, and you then choose a course of action directed toward some objective that you hope will satisfy that need. In short, *need leads to a strategic choice of action directed toward an objective.*

Let's take an example from a scene from *A Raisin in the Sun.* We begin with the given circumstances: it is morning on a work day in the tiny, crowded kitchen of the Lee apartment; as usual, Ruth is fixing breakfast for her husband, Walter. The night before, Walter's friend Willy suggested a scheme to open a liquor store. Willy's idea was that Walter, Willy, and another friend (Bobo) would each invest $10,000 to open the store; it is no coincidence that Walter's father has recently died, leaving a $10,000 life insurance payment; Willy knows this and has concocted the whole scheme (as we will learn later) in order to cheat Walter out of his money. But for now, Walter thinks the scheme is legitimate, and he comes in to breakfast, having decided that he wants to invest the insurance money in Willy's scheme. First, however, Walter knows he must overcome the objections of his devout mother (Mama) who wants nothing to do with a liquor store, and who has other plans for the money. Walter has decided to persuade his wife, Ruth, to approach Mama on his behalf.

Looking at the play as a whole, we see that Walter has a deep overall need to win respect and self-esteem. Walter has chosen the objective of starting a liquor store as the action he hopes will satisfy that need. In this particular scene, that larger objective takes the immediate form of persuading Ruth to intercede with Mama.

Ruth, however, resists. Walter tries several strategies to win her over, each of which is a separate *unit of action* or *beat*; he tries *to make her feel guilty* by reminding her that he missed a similar opportunity once before; he tries *to shame her* into "supporting her man"; he *pleads* with her to save him from his despair. Each of these specific actions is driven by his need to win her over, and that need, in turn, is driven by his deep need to win self-esteem. (In terms we will develop and explore in later steps, Walter's *beat objectives* are strategies driven by his *scene objective*, which, in turn, is driven by his *superobjective*.)

Ruth, for her part, is driven by the need to deal with her secret pregnancy, which at this point she plans to terminate. She mistrusts Walter's friends (with good reason) and dislikes the shady aspects of Walter's scheme (which involves bribing city officials). What she most emphatically does *not* need at this moment is to be drawn into one of Walter's harebrained schemes. Her needs are in direct conflict with Walter's needs (a common and effective dramatic situation) and she finally explodes by telling him, "Then go to work," which has the subtextual meanings of "stop your whining," "do the right thing," and "leave me alone!"

You see that in each instance, the need is *internal* (inside the character) while the objective is *external* ("out there" in the other character). The need causes each character to form an objective, which is then pursued through a strategic action directed toward the other character. We say "strategic" action because the action chosen is one the character thinks will succeed; it is a strategy aimed at achieving the objective. In Walter's case, when trying to make Ruth feel guilty fails, he switches to shaming her, then to pleading. In this case none of these strategies work.

Each character's action is a conduit through which energy flows from need toward objective, and when that action collides with the energy of the other character, it provokes a response in him or her, and so the scene moves forward, interaction by interaction.

You can see that we come to understand a character's needs through his or her actions. Actors sometimes make the mistake of trying to "play" needs: they try to *show* us how much they need self-esteem, how much they need to be left alone, and so on. But as you already know, this results in *indicating*, in *showing* instead of *doing*. Trust that the writer has constructed the character so that the character's actions (what the character says and does) springs naturally from his or her needs; it will be much more satisfying for the audience to figure those needs out for themselves, rather than for you to "show" them what they are.

EXERCISE 12.1: NEEDS (FOURTH READ-THROUGH)

1. Examine the entire play from which your scene comes: does your character have some deep-seated, overall need that drives his or her actions throughout the play?
2. How does this one overall need manifest itself within your scene? What are the immediate and specific needs driving your character within this scene?
3. Read through the scene with your partner; do the needs of your characters conflict with each other? How can you maximize this conflict?
4. Do you have needs that are similar to those of your character? Can you begin to imagine yourself in the character's place, needing the same things?

Trust that you possess a vast personal potential. If you can engage your own energy in your character's actions within the scripted world, and make that world and those actions real for yourself, even if they are unfamiliar, you will find yourself naturally transformed toward a new state of being. In other words, acting is as much *self-expansion* as it is *self-expression*. This expansion, this exploration of new states of being, is the most exciting aspect of the actor's creative process.

Emotional Recall and Substitution

If you encounter a character whose needs or circumstances are so unfamiliar that you have difficulty experiencing them, you might try two techniques designed to help you to connect material from your own life to your work. These techniques are *emotional recall* and *substitution*.

Stanislavski experimented with the idea that the actor could develop a wealth of emotional memories as a resource for the acting process, much as a painter learns to mix colors:

> The broader your emotion memory, the richer your material for inner creativeness. . . . Our creative experiences are vivid and full in direct proportion to the power, keenness and exactness of our memory. . . . Sometimes memories continue to live in us, grow and become deeper. They even stimulate new processes and either fill out unfinished details or suggest altogether new ones.[1]

There are several techniques by which stored memories may be recalled. One of the easiest of these techniques is *visualization*. This involves relaxing deeply and imagining yourself in the character's world, with all its sights, sounds, smells, physical sensations, and so on. Imagine yourself in your character's situation, with all the feelings and needs it involves. From these imagined experiences, you can invite associations from your store of personal memories. These associations, or *recalls*, automatically become attached to the character's actions

---

[1]Stanislavski, *An Actor's Handbook*, trans. and ed. Elizabeth Reynolds Hapgood (New York: Theatre Arts Books, 1936), p. 56. Copyright © 1936, 1961, 1963 by Elizabeth Reynolds Hapgood.

and situation. It is neither necessary nor desirable to "play" them; simply allow them to influence you.

The key to this technique is relaxation. When we relax, our storehouse of memory and subconscious material becomes more accessible. You may notice that when you do relaxation exercises such as meditation, memories often naturally flood up.

Another technique that may be useful in certain situations involves making a mental *substitution* of some situation or some person from your own life for the situation or characters in the scene. If, for example, you are expected to be terribly afraid of another character, it might be useful to recall some frightening person from your own life and substitute that person in your own mind for the other character. Such a substitution will often arise naturally as you form associations between the world of the character and your own experience.

Of course, such emotional recalls and substitutions need not be rooted in real events; fantasy sometimes supplies more powerful material than real life. Your dreams and imagination already provide a storehouse of situations and characters that are as useful in your acting as anything from your real life.

A word of caution: as useful as emotional recalls and substitutions may sometimes be, they can also be dangerous. First, memories can be very powerful and can *overwhelm artistic control*. Second, recalls and substitutions can become *obstacles between you and your scene partners;* it is awful to be on stage with someone who is looking at you with a vacant stare because he or she is "seeing" someone else in his or her own mind or is busy reliving the day the family dog died. Third, and most dangerous, the emotional power of recalls may distract you from your focus on your objective and lure you into *playing an emotional state*. For all these reasons, recalls and substitutions may be carefully used in rehearsal but are absolutely *not* intended for use in performance. Stanislavski himself eventually abandoned these techniques entirely.

EXERCISE 12.2: PERSONALIZATION (LAST READ-THROUGH)

1. Place yourself comfortably at rest and take a few deep breaths to relax.
2. Now go through your scene mentally; picture the entire circumstance and live through your character's actions as if you were actually doing them in those circumstances. Let your body respond freely. (This technique, used by Olympic athletes with great success, is called *visuo-motor-behavior rehearsal* [VMBR].)
3. As you live through the scene in your mind, notice the emotional associations that arise. Do you remember events from your past? Do the other characters remind you of people you have known? Let yourself relive these memories fully.
4. Review this exercise and evaluate any connections that were made. Are they useful to the scene? Do they need to be altered to meet the exact demands of the scene?
5. With your partner, read through your scene in front of the group. Allow these associations to influence you, but avoid indicating them.

6. After the reading, discuss it with the group. Were you able to endow your character's need, situation, and action with personal significance? Did the character seem more real to the group? Are you beginning to feel a transformation into the character?

By now, you are well on your way to having your scene memorized; subsequent exercises will require that you have your lines thoroughly memorized. We call this getting "off book." Begin now to get completely off book; have your partner or someone else cue you. You will find that the more fully you understand your character's actions, the easier it will be to learn your lines, which are driven by those actions.

Summary of Step 12

Action is a response to a need; need leads to a choice of strategic action, chosen in relation to the given circumstances, directed toward an objective that will, it is hoped, satisfy the need. The need is internal, but the objective is external. The character's energy is flowing out toward the objective, and this propels the scene forward. Your job is not to show the audience what the need is (*indicating*) but rather to experience the character's needs as if they were your own. You do this by *personalizing* the character's needs, putting yourself in his or her place and making the character's needs and experiences your own. Besides your natural ability to empathize with your character, there are several techniques that can help in doing this, such as recalling emotional experiences and relationships from your own life. These techniques may be part of your personal preparation but they are *not* meant to be used in performance because they may distance you from the scene and your partners.

13 Exploring Inner Action

You already know that your character serves his or her dramatic function through action, by doing and saying certain things in certain ways so as to move the story forward and give it the proper meaning. The writer created your character so these actions are believable and natural to the role. One of the most important aspects of your job is to discover the inner process of thought that lies behind these external actions.

A novelist can take you inside a character's mind to explain what the person is thinking, but a dramatist can only *imply* the character's thought through the character's words and actions. Beginning with those words and actions, you have to recreate the mental processes that produce them. This is what Stanislavski called *justifying* the outer action by connecting it to an inner process. This will be the greatest creative and personal contribution you will make to your performance, and it will be the foundation of all the other work you do on the role.

Let's examine the connection between inner and outer action in detail. Think back to the impulse circle exercise (3.1). The slap you received was a *stimulus*—it aroused you, caused a *reaction* as it passed through you, and then left you as an *action* as you slapped the next person's hand. Your action then became a stimulus for the next person, generated a reaction, which in turn generated another action, and so the slap moved around the circle. Similarly, a dramatic scene moves as the characters react and act to one another. *Reaction turns into action*, forming the flow of action—reaction—action—reaction that moves the story forward.

The impulse circle exercise was not exactly like a scene, of course. In the exercise, the slap was more or less the same as it moved around the circle. After a while, that would become repetitious and boring. In a dramatic scene, the energy leaving each character as action is not the same as the energy that enters as stimulus; it is altered as it passes through each character by his or her needs, personality, and objectives. So in a scene on stage, the "slap" is continually changing as the story evolves, and this makes it more interesting and suspenseful.

From this, you can see that each character is a channel through which the energy of the story flows and that each character contributes something special to the changing nature of that energy as the story unfolds. *The inner thought process of each character is designed to produce the proper effect on each link of the flow of reaction—action.* In this step you will explore what happens inside you as your reaction to a stimulus turns into an action directed toward an objective, so as to produce the action needed at that moment to move the story forward properly.

Let's begin to examine this psychological aspect of action by setting up a hypothetical situation: imagine that you see a notice that I am directing a play, and there is a part in this play that you want very badly. Even though you fear possible rejection, your need is strong enough that you come to audition. Consider each step in the formation of this action. First, you saw the notice, which was your *stimulus.* Although you wanted the part, you were also afraid of being rejected; these mixed feelings were your *attitude.* Your need was strong enough to overcome your fear, so after *considering* your alternatives, you *chose* an *action* directed toward an *objective:* you came to audition and tried to persuade me to cast you. (By the way, you got the part!)

This example illustrates the internal process by which action is formed: a *stimulus* arouses you and generates an *attitude,* which generates a *consideration of alternatives,* leading to a *strategic choice* of an *action* directed toward an *objective.* This thought process is represented graphically in Figure 13.1. In this figure, the large circle represents the boundary between your "inner" world and the "outer" world. The *stimulus* enters you through perception (seeing, hearing, touching). It arouses a response in you that carries some *attitude*—it may excite or frighten or please or anger you. At this point, your action may become *automatic,* or it may generate a *strategic choice.* The chosen action may then be either *direct, indirect,* or *suppressed.* Let's look at each step in this process.

The Stimulus and Attitude

The process of inner action begins with real hearing and seeing as you learned in Step 7. Though this seems obvious, some actors only pretend to hear or see what is said or done to them; they fear that if they let the other characters truly affect them, they will lose control of their performances. Instead of trusting and opening up to the other actors, they prefer the safety of reacting only to their own ideas of what the other characters will say and do. It is as if they are responding to a prerecorded, premeditated image of the other actor inside their own heads. When this happens, the performance becomes false and mechanical. Any stimulus generates an *attitude*; it may be frightening, exciting, shocking, and so on. Ask yourself, "What does this mean to me? How do I feel about it?" Of course, beware of indicating your attitude; simply allow yourself to react in that way as if for the first time.

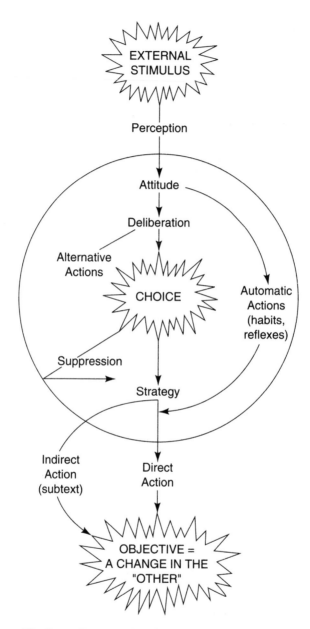

FIGURE 13.1   The Inner Process of Action.

Actors have to depend on each other to provide what every one of them—and the scene itself—needs to move the story forward, moment by moment, as a real human event. Each must supply the required stimuli, and each must truly receive the stimuli provided. Although this doesn't always happen, we strive to achieve this ideal working relationship of real giving and taking. Don't let fear turn you into a hermetically sealed actor. Remember: acting is not so much doing things as it is allowing yourself to be *made* to do them. Again, *acting is reacting!*

Automatic and Spontaneous Actions

As in real life, dramatic characters often act out of habit or impulse; in such cases, the stimulus leads directly to external action without conscious thought (see the arrow bypassing "CHOICE" in Figure 13.1). This is what Stanislavski called *automatic* action. When the slap in the impulse circle was moving quickly, it was an automatic action, something you did without thinking. Likewise, some of the things your character does will be done automatically or unconsciously. We commonly call this unconscious behavior *habit.*

When approaching a part, it is extremely useful to identify the habitual aspects of your character's behavior as soon as possible. You will want to strive to recreate the character's habits in yourself (only for purposes of playing the role, of course). Much of a character's behavior may be habitual: voice, walk, mannerisms, any special skills, or physical qualities. All this will, through repeated rehearsal and homework, become as natural and habitual to you as it is to your character. This takes time, and there is no substitute for practice.

Besides exhibiting habitual character traits, your character may also experience important moments in which he or she is taken unawares by something and reacts automatically—moments of surprise or shock, or moments when the character suddenly understands or recognizes something. For example, in the sample scene from *Cheers*, in Appendix A, Carla begins with a vague feeling that she cannot marry Ben Ludlow, but she does not know exactly why. At first, she thinks it is because he won't want her once he knows the truth about her children, but she soon discovers that he is willing to accept that. And yet, she can't bring herself to say yes.

> LUDLOW: I still haven't heard you say yes.
>
> CARLA: I know. [*Genuinely puzzled*] Why do you think that is?
>
> LUDLOW: I think if you examine your feelings, you'll know.
>
> CARLA: Yeah, I guess I know. I love somebody else.

Just before she says, "Yeah, I guess I know," she has what Aristotle called a *recognition* about the "dream man" in her mind. This has to be a moment of *spontaneous* self-insight. Such moments cannot be mechanically recreated; they must happen afresh every time. In a sense, you have to forget what you are going to discover, then let yourself find it anew. (This does not mean, however, that the form of the moment will vary wildly; you can learn to let it happen within parameters that serve the performance.)

EXERCISE 13.1: AUTOMATIC ACTIONS

Review your scene with your partner.

1. Does your character have any habitual traits? What do these things tell you about your character? What can you do to develop these habits in yourself for this role?
2. Are there moments of recognition, surprise, or impulse that must be spontaneous?

Strategic Choice

In Figure 13.1, you see that if an action is not automatic or spontaneous, then a conscious process of thought begins. The first step is to consider various things you might do. During this *deliberation,* one course of action is chosen and others are rejected. In order to fully experience this process, it may be useful to create the alternative choices that your character rejects. This can be your own special way of personalizing the character's inner world, and it can help you fully experience each choice your character makes. In other words, it may be as important for you to decide what your character *chooses not to do* as it is to know what he or she *does.* After all, you can't really live through a choice unless you have real alternatives. Be sure to live through the choice every time you perform it, or it may start to become automatic.

Notice that choice is at the center of the inner process. Before the choice, energy is moving *into* you; after the choice, energy is moving *out* of you. In other words, *choice is the point at which reaction turns into action.* Because choice is the moment at which reaction turns into action, it is the essence of drama. The most suspenseful moments in stories occur when a character confronts a significant and difficult choice and we wonder "What will he or she do?"

Choice is also the most revealing and expressive point in the process of action. In the making of significant choices, your character is influenced by his or her needs, ways of seeing the world, relationships, beliefs, and values. *If you can experience all the factors influencing your character's most significant choices, you will be in touch with everything needed to create the character's mind.*

Your experience of your character's significant choices is also the main way the Magic If produces transformation in you. When you have entered into your character's circumstances and felt his or her needs, and then have truly lived through his or her choices, action will follow naturally, and with it will come transformation.

Of course, not every choice your character makes is to be given the weight of the significant choices we have been discussing here. In a typical scene, there will be only one or two such significant choices; in an entire role, there may be one singular choice that stands out above all the rest. In the scene from *Cheers*, for example, Carla's main choice is to not marry Ben, whereas Ben's main choice is to accept Carla's rejection with grace. Everything that is said and done in the scene either leads to or flows from these two crucial choices.

The Inner Monologue

Experiencing the process whereby your character forms his or her actions is the most important step toward transformation. Here is a good general rule: whatever your character *doesn't* need to think about needs to be automatic or spontaneous for you as well; whatever your character *does* need to think about, you must think through each and every time you perform the scene.

As a detailed example of this process of inner action, consider this exchange between Amanda and Laura from a scene in *The Glass Menagerie*. Amanda has just discovered that her daughter has not been going to her classes at a business college; she is very upset because she had hoped Laura could have a business career, and is thinking about what else Laura can do.

> **AMANDA:**   Girls that aren't cut out for business careers usually wind up married to some nice man. *[She gets up with a spark of revival.]* Sister, that's what you'll do!
>
> *[Laura utters a startled, doubtful laugh. She reaches quickly for a piece of glass.]*
>
> **LAURA:**   But, Mother—
>
> **AMANDA:**   Yes? *[She goes over to the photograph.]*
>
> **LAURA:**   *[In a tone of frightened apology]*: I'm—crippled!

Laura reaching for the glass animal is an automatic action, something she does every time she feels threatened, a retreat into her "safe" illusory world. But she also tries to deal with the situation in a conscious way, and her internal thought process might sound like this:

1. *Stimulus.* "Married?" Can she really be thinking that?
2. *Attitude.* But no one would want to marry me.
3. *Alternatives.* I could just hide (*reaching for the glass animal*) but I know what Mother is like once she makes up her mind.
4. *Choice.* I've got to talk her out of it.
5. *Action.* "But mother—" "I'm—crippled!"
6. *Objective.* To make her see that her plan is impossible.

You can see that Laura's needs, values, way of thinking, way of relating to the world—in short, her entire psychology—is involved and expressed in each step of this mental process.

Giving words to the internal thought process in this way is called the *inner monologue*. You can purposefully create such a detailed inner monologue as part of your preparation for a role, and it can help you to specify and experience your understanding of your character's process of thought. In performance, this process of thought will once again become intuitive and nearly instantaneous.

Such a highly detailed view of your character's inner thought process may be useful for highly significant choices, but it is too cumbersome to use on a moment-by-moment basis. By simplifying the process, you can achieve an easy formula that you can apply as you rehearse. Break the process into three basic steps: the stimulus, need, and attitude forms the first step, which is called *arousal*; the consideration of alternatives and the choice of a strategic action is the second step, which constitutes the *choice*; finally, the external activity directed toward your objective is the *action*. So your inner process can be summarized by three key words:

Arousal–Choice–Action

You can apply this system by asking yourself three questions about each of the transactions in a scene:

1. What am I reacting to?
2. What does it make me want?
3. What do I do to try to get it? What *don't* I do?

EXERCISE 13.2: CHOICES (FIRST REHEARSAL OFF BOOK)

1. Answer the three questions above about each of your character's actions in your scene.
2. Choose the most significant choice your character makes in the scene and examine it in detail. Create the inner monologue that expresses your character's mental process for this choice. Try writing down the inner monologue.
3. Rehearse your scene with your partner. Take the time to experience each choice fully.
4. Perform the memorized scene for the group and discuss it. Were the moments of choice clear and believable?

Summary of Step 13

The greatest creative and personal contribution you will make to your performance is to discover the inner process of thought that lies behind your character's external actions; this is called *justifying* the action. In the internal process by which action is formed, a *stimulus* is received which generates an *attitude*. The stimulus may lead directly to external action without conscious choice as an *automatic* action. If an action is not automatic, however, a conscious thought process begins with a consideration of alternatives, called *deliberation*. Next, a *strategic choice* is made about the best way to proceed in the given circumstances. *Choice is the point at which reaction turns into action* and from choice comes an *action* directed toward an *objective*.

Giving words to this inner thought process is called the *inner monologue*. A simplified form of the process can be summed up as Arousal–Choice–Action. Ask yourself three questions about each of your actions:

1. What am I reacting to?
2. What does it make me want?
3. What do I do to try to get it? What *don't* I do?

STEP

14 Defining Objectives and Actions

Baseball batters rehearse their stance, grip, swing, and breathing. They study the opposing pitchers. At the plate, they take note of the wind and the position of the fielders. As they begin to swing at a pitch, however, they cease to be aware of all these things and focus their total awareness on the ball. This single objective causes them to channel all their energy into their action, the swing. Having this single objective allows the batter to synthesize all his or her other concerns, and rehearsed and intuitive skills, into a single complete action of mind and body that has tremendous power.

For you as an actor, the "ball" is your character's objective, what he or she is trying to accomplish at any given moment. Your focus on this single objective at the moment of action will overcome self-consciousness and give you power and control. In this step, you will learn how to define your character's objectives (what he or she wants) and actions (what he or she does to try to get it) in the most useful way.

Defining Useful Objectives

Experience has proven that objectives become more effective when they have three main qualities:

1. An objective needs to be *singular* because you need to focus your energy on one thing rather than diffuse it by trying to do several things at once. Imagine a batter trying to hit two balls at the same time!
2. The most useful objective is in the present, something you want *right now*. Although your character's needs may be rooted in the past and may be a step toward some larger, overall objective in the future, his or her action at this moment is directed toward an objective in the immediate present.
3. Finally, an objective must be *personally important* to you. As you have already learned, you must personalize it; this will energize you and make your action powerful.

It is easy to remember these three requirements by the acronym SIP: *singular*, *immediate*, and *personal*.

For example, there is a scene in *Death of a Salesman* in which Willy, a traveling salesman who is having trouble driving, goes to see his boss, Howard. Willy has an overall *scene objective* of wanting to persuade Howard to give him an assignment in town so that he won't have to drive so much, but he has to pursue this scene objective one step at a time, through *immediate objectives*. When he enters, he sees Howard playing with a new recorder, so Willy's *immediate objective* is to get Howard to stop playing with the recorder and to pay attention.

This objective is *singular* and *immediate*. It is also supremely important in a *personal* way to Willy: if he can't get Howard's attention, he won't be able to ask for a job in town; if he doesn't get a job in town, he won't be able to be a successful salesman; if he can't be a successful salesman, he won't think of himself as a valuable human being. In this way, Willy's deepest, lifelong need for self-esteem lives in the present moment, and getting Howard's attention has all the urgency of a life and death struggle.

From this example, you can see that objectives work on three levels: *immediate* objectives are steps toward the *scene* objective, and the scene objective is a step toward the character's life goal, which we call his or her *superobjective* (more about this in the next step). Your character will have one immediate objective within each beat of the scene; when characters in the scene change their objectives, or change the strategy they are using to achieve their objectives, each change creates a new beat (unit of action). A *beat change* can be felt as a change in the flow of the action, because the action of the scene "turns a corner" and moves in a new direction at that point.

Playable Strategic Actions

Since your energy must continually flow outward into the scene in order to keep the story moving, you want to define your actions in the most "playable" (that is, *active*) way possible. First, you use a *simple verb phrase in a transitive form*, that is, a verb that involves a *doing* directed *toward* someone else, such as "to flatter him." You avoid forms of the verb *to be* because this verb has no external object and its energy turns back on itself. You are never interested, for example, in "being angry" or "being a victim"; these states of being are not playable. Strive instead for a *doing* in which your energy flows toward an external object.

Next, you select a verb that carries a sense of the particular *strategy* chosen by your character to achieve the objective. As in real life, your character will naturally select an action that seems to offer the greatest chance for success in the given circumstances and in relation to the other person in the scene.

Let's return to the Willy Loman scene and see how you might describe your action if you were playing Willy. You have just entered; you desperately need to get a spot in town; you see Howard playing with the recorder. At this moment, you have the SIP objective of getting Howard to pay attention, but you want to do it in a way that will make him feel positively toward you. As a salesman, you instinctively appeal to something the "client" is interested in, so you flatter him by praising the recorder and the stupid recording he has made of his family. The most complete description of your action and objective at this moment is *to flatter Howard by praising the recorder* (strategic action) in order *to get him to pay attention to me in a positive way* (objective).

While you are learning to act, it may help you to form such a complete verbal description of your objectives and actions. Remember, however, that these verbal descriptions are valuable only insofar as they contribute to your actual experience of playing the scene. The ability to describe something comes from the analytical left side of the brain, whereas the creative work of performance originates from the intuitive right side of the brain. Although they can complement and augment one another wonderfully, the two sometimes get in each other's way.

EXERCISE 14.1: DEFINING OBJECTIVES AND ACTIONS

Go through your scene and define each of your objectives and actions.

1. Make each objective SIP.
2. Describe each action with a transitive verb phrase that expresses the strategy being used.

Direct and Indirect Action: Subtext

We have already seen that a character will select an action that seems to offer the best chance for success in the given circumstances. As in real life, characters will often select a direct action such as persuading, demanding, cajoling, or begging. However, sometimes there is an obstacle to direct action. An obstacle to direct action may be *internal*, like Willy's fear of angering Howard, or *external*, like Howard's obsession with the recorder. At such times, the character will, as people do in everyday life, try to get around the obstacle through an indirect approach.

When we act indirectly, we say or do one thing but really mean another. Although Willy *seems* to be enjoying Howard's recording, he actually wants to get Howard to turn it off and pay attention. This kind of "hidden agenda" creates a *subtext*, because there is a difference between the surface activity (the text) and the hidden objective (the subtext).

How do you play a subtext? *You don't!* Notice that the writer has provided a surface activity through which the subtext may be expressed—in this case, your feigned interest in the recorder. You must accept this surface activity as your immediate action: do not attempt to bring the subtext to the surface of the scene by indicating it. Doing so will destroy the reality of the scene. For one thing, if the audience can see Willy's subtext, they will wonder why Howard can't. Your simple awareness of subtext is enough, and often subtext will work even if you are unaware of it.

Trust the audience to deduce the subtext from the situation. It is part of the fun for the audience to figure these things out for themselves; if you make it obvious, they won't get to use their imaginations!

EXERCISE 14.2: SUBTEXT

Examine the objectives you defined in the previous exercise: do any of them involve an *indirect* strategy?

1. If so, why can't the action be expressed directly? What is the obstacle?
2. Is the obstacle, if any, internal or external?
3. Does your character therefore have a subtext or hidden agenda?
4. What is the surface action? Rehearse the scene with your partner. Can you experience the subtext without bringing it to the surface of the scene?

Not Doing

There is always at least one alternative available to a character in any situation, and that is the choice to *not* act—to suppress or delay action. There is a wonderful scene in the middle of Shakespeare's *Hamlet*, for instance, in which Hamlet decides *not* to kill Claudius despite a perfect opportunity to do so. Although we often think of such "not doing" as passivity, it can actually be a strong form of action because it takes more effort to hold a strong impulse in than it would to let it out. As you can see in Figure 13.1 on page 88, when a character chooses to suppress an impulse, that unresolved energy is reflected back into that character and builds up to become a source of increasing dynamic tension.

In everyday life we call this choice to not do *suppression*, which literally means "pushing down." Viewed in this way, there are no passive characters on the stage or screen, there are only characters who are aroused but then choose *not* to act. Because the writer can only infer suppressed actions from the context, you will have to use your imagination to discover them. Examine your scene beat by beat and ask yourself, is there anything my character wants to do here but doesn't?

The choice to not act is a strong and playable action. To play a "not doing," simply identify what the character *wants* to do but *doesn't*. Let yourself feel the need to act strongly and feel also the effort required to suppress the action. This process turns the "not doing" into a "doing" and makes it playable and dramatic.

EXERCISE 14.3: SUPPRESSION

Work through your scene with your partner. Look for any suppressed actions. Discuss any you find. Read through your scene with this awareness: avoid indicating the suppressed actions, but allow yourself to experience them fully.

Obstacles and Counter-Actions

Since plays, films, and TV shows are about people interacting dramatically with one another, you must understand your objectives in ways that not only energize and focus you by being SIP and transitive, but also connect you with the other characters in the scene. The best way to achieve connectedness is to think of your objective as being *in* the other character, something specific you need from that person. The best objective, then, is *a change you want to bring about in the other character.*

In life, when we do something to try to make a change in someone else, we watch to see if what we are doing is working; if it is not, we try something else. This should be true on stage as well. Ask yourself, "How would I know I was achieving my objective? What changes might I see in the other character that indicate that my approach is working?"

This sort of observable change that you want to bring about in the other character is the best way to define your objective. One acting teacher even encouraged his actors to think of their objective as "a change in the other character's eyes." In the Willy Loman scene, for instance, your first objective might be *to get Howard to look at me with interest.* Your full attention is on him, watching to see if your behavior is indeed producing the desired effect, or whether you might have to try a different approach (which in this case you eventually do).

Notice how each of your objectives affects the other character and vice versa. You are each evoking a reaction in the other, and you may also be presenting *obstacles* to one another's actions. In the most extreme cases, your objectives may be in direct contradiction, and you may be acting *counter* to one another. Howard's insistence that Willy listen to the recording of his family, for example, is a *counter-action* to Willy's attempts to get Howard's attention. It is likely, in fact, that Howard is deliberately using the recording to avoid Willy. Such obstacles and counter-actions are important to the development of the drama of a scene, and by playing *into* one another you get full value from them.

> ### EXERCISE 14.4: CONNECTING THE ACTION (SECOND REHEARSAL OFF BOOK)
>
> 1. Go through your scene and define each of your objectives as a change in the other character.
> 2. Identify how your characters provide obstacles and counter-actions to one another so as to heighten drama.
> 3. Rehearse the scene with this awareness. Did you achieve a stronger interaction? Did the action of the scene flow better?

Summary of Step 14

The best focus of awareness for an actor is the character's objective (what he or she wants) from which flows the character's action (what he or she does to try to get it). This focus on a single objective at the moment of action will overcome self-consciousness and give you power and control.

Objectives become more effective when they are SIP: *singular, immediate,* and *personal.* Actions are best defined actively, using a *simple verb phrase in a transitive form.* Avoid forms of the verb "to be" because their energy turns back upon itself. Your verb should reflect the particular *strategy* chosen by your character to achieve the objective.

When there is an *internal* or *external* obstacle that prevents direct action, characters may try to get around the obstacle through an indirect approach; this kind of hidden agenda is a *subtext.* Never try to bring the subtext to the surface! A character may also choose to *not* act, to *suppress* action, and this helps to build suspense.

It is best to think of an objective as *a change you want to bring about in the other character.* Drama is heightened when characters present obstacles and counter-actions to one another.

STEP

15 Finding the Scenario,
Score, Through-Line,
and Superobjective

Remember what you learned about units of actions, or beats, in Steps 9 and 14: a beat consists of several interactions between characters and is driven by a conflict that comes from the action of one character encountering the resistance (or even counter-action) of another. Like people in everyday life, dramatic characters will pursue actions until they either succeed or fail. If their actions succeed and they achieve their objectives, they move on to new objectives and actions; if they decide their actions are not working, they will try different strategies and form new actions (for example, if *persuading* doesn't work, they may switch to *demanding*). The moment in which a character changes action causes a change in the flow of the scene as a new beat begins. We call each of these moments a *beat change*. We feel the rhythm of the scene as it flows from beat to beat toward the crisis, when the main conflict of the scene may be resolved, or if it is not resolved, we move on to the next step in the evolving story.

This structure is not an arbitrary choice made by the actors: it is built into the structure of the scene by the writer, although there is often room for interpretation as the actors develop their own sense of how the action flows. Every actor in a scene works to contribute to the structure of the scene, and each of them supports the beat changes when they occur, even when the particular change is not initiated by his or her character.

An analysis of the structure of a scene, beat by beat, is called a "scene breakdown" or *scenario*. As an example of a scenario, let's look again at the scene from *A Raisin in the Sun* we discussed in Step 12 on page 81: Walter begins the scene with the *scene objective* of persuading Ruth to go to Mama with the plan for a liquor store suggested to him by his friend, Willy. As Ruth resists him, he tries a number of different strategies to achieve this objective, each of which is a new action and therefore a new beat.

1. Walter begins by trying *to arouse Ruth's curiosity* about what he has been thinking about. She refuses to rise to the bait ("I know what you thinking 'bout.") and when he tells her anyway, she immediately cuts him off ("Willy Harris is a good-for-nothing loud mouth.").

2. Faced with her resistance, Walter switches strategy and defends his friends, trying *to shame her* by reminding her that she cost him his chance for a successful business once before. Ruth responds by collapsing in exhaustion.

3. Walter reacts by saying that he is tired too, and switches to the strategy of trying *to make her do her duty as a wife* because "A man needs for a woman to back him up . . . " and "Mama would listen to you." He outlines in detail how she could successfully approach Mama, ending by reminding her of her place as a woman ("See there, that just goes to show you what women understand about the world.").

4. The scene now reaches its crisis as Ruth counterattacks ("Walter, leave me alone!"). Walter retreats into self-pity, making one last effort *to shame her* into joining his plan by pleading that he must change his life for the sake of their son. Again she resists with "Eat your eggs, Walter."

5. He angrily admits defeat with an emotional outburst, and she counters with "Then go to work," which carries the subtext "Do something realistic and give up this stupid liquor store idea."

Doing a scenario in this way reveals the power struggle underlying a scene. Here, Ruth is on the defensive and Walter initiates the beat changes until she finally counterattacks. When you add to this an understanding of Ruth's hidden pain (that she is thinking of terminating her secret pregnancy) and how much Walter's irresponsibility adds to her dilemma, you see that her seemingly simple responses carry a huge emotional weight.

Understanding the scenario of a scene greatly simplifies it for you. This scene, for example, can be understood as having just three beats leading to its crisis, followed by one beat of follow-through. Most importantly, notice that within each beat each character has *a single objective and action.* This fact permits you to translate the structure of the scene into the thoughts and actions of your character, through an understanding of how the inner action of your character contributes to the structure and flow of the scene, moment by moment.

EXERCISE 15.1: SCENARIO (THIRD REHEARSAL OFF BOOK)

1. Working with your partner, come to a mutual agreement about where the overall crisis of the scene occurs. Then prepare a scenario by agreeing on where each beat change happens.

2. On your own, define your character's action and objective in each beat, whether you initiate the beat change or not. Remember to express each action as a transitive verb that is SIP, and think of each objective as a desired change in the other character.

3. Rehearse the scene together to emphasize and clarify the rhythms of the beat changes.

4. Perform the scene in front of the group; ask the group to note where they feel the beats changing, and where they feel the crisis of the entire scene to be. Afterward, compare their response to your scenario.

The Score

Rehearsing a scene in this way is much like making a map of an unknown territory. You and your partner, through trial and error, explore it to find the pathway of action that the author has hidden beneath the surface of the dialogue. Each beat change is a turning point in the journey leading to the destination, the scene crisis. Once you and your partner have found a shared sense of the scene's structure, it will live as an underlying rhythm in the flow of the scene, and you will feel the energy building beat by beat toward the crisis, then flowing from it.

As your exploration of the scene in rehearsal develops, you begin to feel how the sequence of your character's objectives has a logical flow that can carry you through the scene with a natural momentum. Stanislavski called this sequence of objectives the *score* of the role:

> With time and frequent repetition, in rehearsal and performance, this score becomes habitual. An actor becomes so accustomed to all his objectives and their sequence that he cannot conceive of approaching his role otherwise than along the line of the steps fixed in the score. . . . The score automatically stirs the actor to physical action.[1]

This sense of the underlying structure of the scene will help you in many ways. For one, it will make it easier to learn your lines. As one of my actor friends says, he likes to "learn the action" before he "learns the words."

More importantly, a good sense of scene structure is the "map" that permits the actors to support one another in their journey through the scene. The "map" helps to lessen your fear of becoming lost, making your work more playful and creative; it also helps you to experience the scene as a single, rhythmic event. One symptom that the scene has started to "play" in this way is that it will seem shorter to you; it is this natural flow of action that we call good *pace*.

Through-Line and Superobjective

You learned in Part Three that a good story is structured on several levels of action: individual interactions make up beats, beats make up scenes, and the scenes form the overall shape of the rising and falling action of the entire story, giving unity to the whole. These levels of action relate directly to the inner life of your character. You will have an objective on each level: in each beat you have a *beat objective*; the beat objectives lead toward your *scene objective*; and your scene objective can be seen as springing from a deep, overall objective that is your character's *superobjective*.

---

[1]Stanislavski, *Creating a Role*, trans. Elizabeth Reynolds Hapggod (New York: Theatre Arts Books, 1961), p. 62.

The idea of the superobjective is easier to grasp if you think of it as a "life goal" or "guiding principle" governing the character's behavior, often on an unconscious level. Think of someone you know well and see if there seems to be a life goal at work in them. Such drives are basic, such as the desire for love, respect, security, or aliveness. They can be "negatives," such as the avoidance of failure or ridicule. They can be idealistic, such as passion for justice or freedom. It is not often easy to identify someone's superobjective unless you have a lot of experience with them and know them well; just so, your understanding of your character's superobjective will develop gradually as you rehearse. Your sense of your character's superobjective is the *result* of your experience of the role, not a prerequisite for it; but it may be useful to form a general idea of the superobjective early on, knowing that it may change as your work progresses.

For example, consider again the scene we have already discussed from *Death of a Salesman*. Willy finds Howard engrossed in his new recorder; at this moment his *beat* objective is to get Howard's attention so he can move toward his *scene* objective of getting an assignment in town. This scene objective is connected directly to Willy's *superobjective:* to be a successful salesman, which for Willy is a way *to prove himself a worthy human being by earning money and respect.* (Notice that defining the superobjective, as defining objectives on any level, requires using a transitive verb.)

If we follow each of Willy's beat and scene objectives throughout the play, we see how in each case he is led from objective to objective in pursuit of his superobjective. The logic of this sequence of objectives striving toward the superobjective is called the *through-line* of the role. Stanislavski described it like this:

> In a play the whole stream of individual minor objectives, all the imaginative thoughts, feelings and actions of an actor should converge to carry out this superobjective. . . . Also this impetus toward the superobjective must be continuous throughout the whole play.[2]

Stanislavski once said that each of a character's actions fits into the through-line like vertebrae in a spine. Therefore, some actors call the through-line the "spine" of the role.

Identifying your character's through-line of action as being driven by his or her superobjective can help you to better understand each of your specific objectives, connecting each to the character's deepest needs and desires. It can also help you to see how the sequence of objectives has a single driving force; thus you can "play through" each moment and achieve both unity and momentum (good *pace*) in your performance.

Your character's superobjective may be conscious or (more commonly) unconscious. If the character is unconscious of it, you—the actor—will have to

---

[2]Stanislavski, *An Actor's Handbook*, trans. and ed. Elizabeth Reynolds Hapgood (New York: Theatre Arts Books, 1936), p. 56. Copyright © 1936, 1961, 1963, by Elizabeth Reynolds Hapgood.

treat it in a special way. You will take it fully into account as you work, but you will not let your knowledge as an actor "contaminate" your character's reality. Remember the idea of dual consciousness: what you know as the actor is not the same thing as what your character knows. The acting teacher Lee Strasberg once said the hardest thing about acting "is not knowing what you know."

Whether or not your character is conscious of his or her superobjective, it functions as an underlying principle that affects all of your actions and establishes your attitude toward life. Willy Loman tries to earn self-esteem through selling; he confuses success as a salesman with success as a human being. Each moment, each beat, each scene, and every aspect of Willy's psychology can be understood as reflecting his superobjective. Eventually, he is no longer able to sell either his products or himself. His last "sale" is his suicide, making the insurance money his last "paycheck." Thus, this final, desperate act (which is the climax of the play) is the fulfillment of Willy's tragically misguided way of pursuing his superobjective.

It is by experiencing how each moment, beat, and scene of your character's behavior is driven by his or her superobjective that you will fulfill what Stanislavski called the actor's main task: to understand how every moment of the performance contributes to the reason the play was written.

Personalizing the Superobjective

Because the superobjective of most major characters is fairly universal, it is usually not difficult to personalize. Like Willy Loman, we all want to be thought of as worthy, and we can all identify with Willy, however much we can see that Willy's way of pursuing self-esteem is mistaken.

You must make the most of any connections you find between your character's goals and your own. There may be characters, however, whose life goals are difficult for you to find in yourself. In these cases, you may be able to substitute some analagous need of your own, or simply use your imaginative skill to create the superobjective in yourself. However you do it, you need to base your work on this kind of deeply personal and real experience of the character's deepest needs and energies.

It may be more difficult to find the superobjective of minor characters, because the writer has not provided much information about them. Here you can be inventive, so long as your understanding of the character enables you to accurately serve your dramatic function within the play as a whole.

The superobjective naturally colors the way a character sees him or herself. Willy's superobjective, for example, is to prove himself worthy by earning money and respect, so his underlying self-image must be that he is *un*worthy as a human being. Much of his behavior seems perversely dedicated to proving his own unworthiness; the self-image is often a self-fulfilling prophecy.

In fact, you may be able to discover the superobjectve by examining your character's attitude toward him- or herself.

EXERCISE 15.2: SELF-IMAGE

1. What is your character's dominant self-image? Enter into your character's frame of mind and complete these phrases:
   a. The most beautiful part of my body is . . .
   b. Happiness to me is . . .
   c. The thing I most want to do before I die is . . .
   d. The ugliest part of my body is . . .
   e. The thing I like best about myself is . . .
   f. Pain to me is . . .
   g. My mother . . .
   h. The most secret thing about me is . . .
   i. I can hear my father's voice speaking through my own when I tell myself . . .
   j. Love to me is . . .
   k. If you could hear the music in me . . .
   l. I want my epitaph to be . . .
2. Immediately work through the scene and allow these feelings to affect you.

Again, avoid the temptation to indicate. It is never your aim to explain your superobjective to the audience. Your job is to create experience, not to explain behavior.

EXERCISE 15.3: THE SUPEROBJECTIVE (FOURTH REHEARSAL OFF BOOK)

1. Examine your character's actions. Can you see a superobjective toward which he or she is striving? Is the character conscious of it?
2. Define the superobjective using a transitive verb phrase.
3. Now consider ways of personalizing this superobjective so that you feel it with the same intensity as does your character. You might even find a line from the play which sums it up: Willy Loman, for example, says, "Be liked and you will never want."
4. Rehearse, then perform your scene for the group. Discuss how the superobjective is expressed in it. Did you avoid indicating?

Summary of Step 15

When a character changes objective or action, it causes a change in the flow of the scene; we call each of these moments a *beat change*. An analysis of the structure of a scene, beat by beat, is called a "scene breakdown" or *scenario*. Doing a scenario often reveals the power struggle between the characters underlying the scene.

You understand now that your character has objectives on three levels: immediate *beat objectives* are derived from the *scene objectives*, and scene objectives spring from a deep, overall objective which is your character's "life goal" or *superobjective.* The logic of the sequence of objectives striving toward the super-objective is called the *through-line* (or "spine") of the role.

Feeling the flow of this sequence of objectives is called the *score* of the role; it can help you to "play through" each moment and achieve both unity and momentum (good *pace*) in your performance. Ideally, the sense of superobjective will emerge gradually from your experience of the specific actions of your character; it is a *result* of your rehearsal exploration, not a substitute for it, and must be felt by you on a deeply personal level.

STEP

16 Preparing for Performance

As you prepare your scene for public performance, you must begin to consider what adjustments may be needed to make your work accessible to an audience. Your first consideration will be the physical and vocal adjustments that may be required by the stage on which you will perform.

The Stage

A stage is defined by its spatial relationship to the audience. There are four basic types of stage configurations: proscenium, thrust, arena, and environmental (see Figure 16.1). Let's consider what each of the basic types means to the actor.

Proscenium

The traditional proscenium stage features an arch through which the audience sees the action. This "picture frame" evolved as a way of establishing a point of reference for settings painted in perspective (hence the word *proscenium* which means "in front of the scene"). The actor on the proscenium stage must, of course, realize that the audience is limited to one side of the playing area, but it is not necessary to "cheat out" continually (to turn your body partly out toward the audience); doing so makes your character look as if he or she is more interested in speaking to the audience than to the other characters in the scene. So while you may make some adjustments because of the audience's location, you must do so without destroying the internal logic of the character's environment. Don't underestimate how much acting you can do with your back.

Thrust

The thrust stage (so called because it "thrusts" into the midst of the audience) features the same stage/audience relationship as the Classical and Elizabethan theaters and places the actor into close proximity with the audience, but also limits the use of scenery. For this reason, it is very much an "actor's" theater. For the actor, there is some added responsibility to keep open to audience view, or at

107

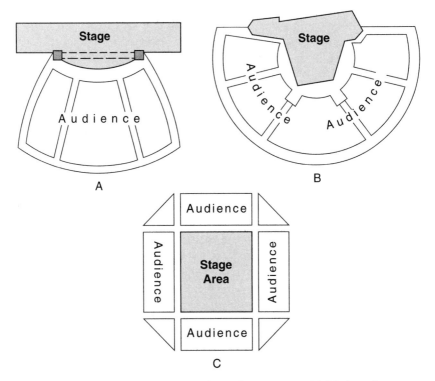

FIGURE 16.1   Types of Stages: (A) Traditional proscenium; (B) Modern thrust;
(C) Arena.

least to distribute his or her presence equally to all sections of the house, but the
increased sense of audience contact inherent in the thrust stage makes such
accommodation easy and natural.

Arena

The arena and other types of full-round or three-quarter round stages stand at
the opposite extreme from proscenium stages. Here the audience surrounds the
stage, so it is important for the actors not to stand too close to one another
because they will block one another from audience view. The arena stage offers
the greatest sense of intimacy of all stage types, and such theaters are usually rel-
atively small. Audiences tend to expect a more detailed and subtle performance
here, something closer to what is required for the camera.

Environmental

While most stages are of the three basic types previously described, we sometimes create special environments for specific productions, some of which may

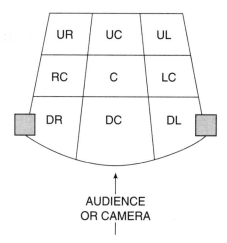

FIGURE 16.2 Locations on a Proscenium Stage.

entirely eliminate the separation of stage and audience. Here, of course, the proximity of the audience demands total commitment and attention to detail, just as the camera does in film acting.

Moving on Stage

When we discuss movement and position on stage, we use a standard nomenclature that you should learn.

Vertical directions are described by very old terms developed for the proscenium at a time when the stage floor was sloped upward away from the audience in order to enhance the illusion of perspective. Even today, moving away from the audience is called going "upstage," and moving toward the audience is going "downstage." To stand "level" with another actor is for both of you to stand perpendicular (in profile) to the audience. (Moving upstage during a scene so that the other actors are forced to turn their backs on the audience in order to speak to you is called "upstaging"; avoid it.)

Lateral directions are determined by the actors' view as they face the audience. Thus "stage right" is the same as the audience's left; "downstage right" means toward the audience and to the actor's right (see Figure 16.2).

Turns are described as being either "in" (toward the center of the stage, whichever side of the stage you are on) or "out" (again, away from center). *Crossing* (that is, moving from one point to another) may be in a straight line, or in a slight arc so that you end facing more in profile to the audience. A cross with an exaggerated arc is called a "circle cross" (or sometimes a "banana").

Positions as you pivot relative to the audience are called "one quarter," "half," and "three-quarters" depending on how far you turn from one side to the other. Thus a director may tell you to "cheat out one-quarter," which means to pivot 45 degrees away from center.

This system of directions can soon become second nature to you.

EXERCISE 16.1: DIRECTIONS ON STAGE

Have your partner stand in the center of the stage and stand beside him or her on the stage right side; your partner will "play director" by giving you the following directions; when you have finished, switch places.

Go down right. / Turn out and go up right. / Take a long cross down left, going upstage of me. / Turn in and do a circle cross up, passing on the downstage side of me and ending level with me on the right. / Cheat out one-quarter. / Circle up to the right around me and exit left center.

Blocking

Blocking is the way in which the characters move in relation to one another and within the space determined by the designer and director of the play. This spatial configuration and the placement of entranceways and objects is called the *groundplan.* Because you don't have a director or designer for your scene to provide a groundplan, you and your partner will have to determine it for yourselves. Keep it simple, with the minimum of furniture or props required by the action.

You have probably already found the basics of the blocking during your earlier rehearsals as you felt the impulse to move in relationship to one another. Build on what you have already discovered; don't feel the need to embellish or add movement just for its own sake. For now, don't be concerned with the onlookers; play directly to one another and don't falsify your relationship by "cheating out" toward the audience. Remember that good blocking always springs from the relationship of the characters and the underlying action of the scene. Blocking at its best expresses things such as: Who is dominant at this moment in the scene? What space does this person control? Who is on whose side? Who is on the attack? Who is retreating? Is there a counterattack?

Although the sense of spatial relationship is artistically heightened on the stage, it is based on the way people relate to one another spatially in everyday life. Look around you and observe how the locations people have taken in the room reflect their relationships and attitudes. Notice how changes in relationship are reflected by movements we make, as we move closer or further away from one another, or change position within the space we share. These are the kinds of impulses you will feel as you experience your action—they are the basis of your blocking. Let yourself move!

EXERCISE 16.2: BLOCKING

1. Spend a few days watching the "blocking" of everyday life; notice how attitude, relationship, and action are expressed in the way people place themselves in a room and move in relationship to each other. Make notes in your journal.
2. After creating a simple groundplan, work with your partner to block the scene; make the blocking an effective expression of the relationship and action in the scene. Follow your impulses.

When you are working with a director, he or she may have various approaches to blocking. Some directors will preplan the blocking in detail, but most directors prefer that the actors provide the impulses that generate the blocking, with the director then editing them as needed. Regardless of what method your director uses, your main responsibility is to *justify* your stage movement so that it grows out of an inner need and expresses your relationship with the other characters in the scene. You may have to supply this justification in your own mind if your director provides a piece of blocking that feels awkward, although many times a director is using the blocking to tell you something about the action. If he or she asks you to "move into her," the director may really be saying, "This is where you counterattack."

Shaping and Pacing

Now that you are well into the rehearsal of your scene, you and your partner are beginning to shape and specify the interactions of action–reaction that form the flow of action that binds the scene together. As you feel the connectedness of every moment with every other moment, your through-line begins to emerge and the scene begins "to play," to flow under its own power. You no longer have to *make* things happen; you can *let* them happen. As a result, your scene begins to feel simpler and shorter. Finding and perfecting these connections is the most important business of your final rehearsals.

EXERCISE 16.3: MAKING CONNECTIONS (FIFTH REHEARSAL OFF BOOK)

Work through your scene with your partner; either of you may stop the rehearsal at any point when you do not feel connected to the flow of the action, when your partner is not "making" you do what you must do next.

At each point of difficulty, examine the moments that led up to it; what do you need from your partner to induce your next action? Work together so that every moment of the scene grows organically out of the flow of action and reaction.

Note: Do not tell your partner what to do; instead, ask for what you *need* and leave it to your partner to provide it. You might, for example, say something like "I need to be more threatened by that" but leave it to your partner to determine how best to threaten you.

In this late stage of rehearsal, each beat change and the scene crisis are brought into sharp focus. Accordingly, the flow of action that connects these elements is established and smoothed to provide a sense of urgency, significance, rising dramatic tension, and the momentum we call good pace. (Note that *pace* refers to the *momentum* of the action, regardless of its *tempo*, which refers to its *speed*.)

One important element of good pace is *cueing*, the way one character begins to speak after another has finished. In real life, if you and I are discussing something, I listen to you in order to understand the idea you are trying to express. When I have grasped the idea, I form my response and am usually ready to begin answering before you have actually finished your sentence. Listen to real-life conversations; do you hear how we sometimes overlap one another's speeches slightly or at least are ready to respond before the other person has stopped talking? This is good "cueing."

> ### EXERCISE 16.4: SHAPING AND PACING THE SCENE (DRESS REHEARSAL)
>
> 1. Provide any simple furniture or props you need and dress appropriately for this final rehearsal.
> 2. Together, find the aspects of the situation that provide the urgency or sense of deadline that will drive the scene's momentum:
>   a. The physical environment: time, place, and so on
>   b. The social environment: customs, the presence of others
>   c. The situation: internal or external factors that create urgency or tension
>   d. The conflict between you
> 3. Practice your listening and responding skills to produce good cueing.

Spontaneity

What you do in performance should feel spontaneous, "as if for the first time," no matter how many times you have done it before. To achieve this spontaneity, you must keep your awareness on your objective rather than on the mechanics of your external action, just as the baseball batter thinks only about the ball and not about his swing. Otherwise you will only be "going through the motions," repeating the external aspects of your performance without re-experiencing the internal needs that drive the externals.

Notice that spontaneity does not mean that your performance is erratic or changeable: during the rehearsal process you gradually refine your external action until it becomes dependable, consistent, stageworthy, and automatic, just as the baseball batter has rehearsed all the aspects of his swing until he can do it without thinking. As Stanislavski said,

A spontaneous action is one that, through frequent repetition in rehearsal and performance, has become automatic and therefore free.[1]

Because you are able to perform your action without thinking about it, your mind is free to concentrate fully on the objective and to experience your action "as if for the first time" in the here and now.

Emotion in Performance

Young actors sometimes think they must recreate the character's emotion in order to generate each performance "truthfully," but this is an exhausting and unreliable way of working. Since emotion arises from action, you need only *do* what your character does and *think* the thoughts involved in the action; the performance itself will then give you the emotion.

We may sometimes be tempted to admire the emotionality of the actor who loses control and is overwhelmed, but the display of emotion for its own sake is never our true purpose. The great actor aspires to use emotional technique to realize the truth of the character according to the demands of the material. Stanislavski said it this way:

> Our art . . . requires that an actor experience the agony of his role, and weep his heart out at home or in rehearsals, that he then calm himself, get rid of every sentiment alien or obstructive to his part. He then comes out on the stage to convey to the audience in clear, pregnant, deeply felt, intelligible and eloquent terms what he has been through. At this point the spectators will be more affected than the actor, and he will conserve all his forces in order to direct them where he needs them most of all: in reproducing the inner life of the character he is portraying.[2]

The important idea here is that in performance, "the spectators will be more affected than the actor." This is necessary for several reasons. First, strong emotion will interfere with your craftsmanship; as Stanislavski put it, "a person in the midst of experiencing a poignant emotional drama is incapable of speaking of it coherently."[3] Second, emotions are unreliable when it comes to generating a performance that must be done repeatedly and on schedule. Stanislavski used the example of the opera singer who, at the moment the music requires a certain note with a certain feeling, cannot say to the conductor, "I'm not feeling it yet, give me four more measures." Finally, if your emotion calls undue attention to

---

[1]Stanislavski, *An Actor's Handbook*, trans. and ed. Elizabeth Reynolds Hapgood (New York: Theatre Arts Books, 1936), p. 138. Copyright © 1936, 1961, 1963 by Elizabeth Reynolds Hapgood.
[2]Stanislavski, *Building a Character*, trans. Elizabeth Reynolds Hapgood (New York: Theatre Arts Books, 1949), p. 70.
[3]Ibid.

itself, you will have failed. As an audience member I am not here to watch you weep; I am here to weep myself.

EXERCISE 16.5: FINAL PERFORMANCE

Present your scene, as fully staged as you are able. Allow yourselves to be spontaneous, and let emotion arise of its own accord. Experience something of the thrill of an opening night.

Evaluating Your Work

The fundamental drives for most actors, like most people, are the desire for success and its flip side, the fear of failure. The desire for success can give you tremendous energy and the courage to take risks, while the fear of failure encourages safe and conservative choices, leading, at best, to technical skill that can never entirely compensate for a lack of creativity.

An excessive fear of failure can cause you to censor creative impulses, fearing that you'll "look foolish," and encourages you to continually judge your own performance to see whether you are "doing it right." This produces self-consciousness and tension. Although a small part of every actor's consciousness is necessarily reserved for ongoing artistic evaluation of the performance, this awareness can only *witness*, not *control*, the performance.

The desire for success carries its own dangers. There are two ways of measuring success: in *internal* terms, such as pride, sense of accomplishment, and feelings of growth, and by *external* measurements, such as reviews, grades, and the response of the audience. Obviously, all actors are concerned with both; what is needed is perspective and balance between the two.

Most actors err on the side of emphasizing external measures of success over internal. Even if they have a sense of their own work, they usually don't trust it, and they feel so dependent on the opinions of others that a negative response from anyone damages their self-esteem. Although it hurts any actor when his or her work is not received well, the serious actor strives to balance the desire for immediate success with the equally important long-range need for artistic development. You should approach each new role, each rehearsal, and each performance with a desire not only to please others, but also to satisfy your own needs, to learn and grow for yourself. When evaluating the experience, you must ask not only, "Did I do the job well?" but also, "Am I now a better human being and a better actor for having done it?"

EXERCISE 16.6: MEASURING SUCCESS

Think back to your performance. Given that all actors have anxiety about performing, did your anxiety stay within controllable levels? Did you experience destructive tension? Did you censor yourself? Did you manage to stay in the moment?

Did you have your own independent evaluation of your performance? Did you trust that evaluation? How did the comments of others affect you?

Did you distinguish between the short-term measurement of your success in the role and the long-term benefits of the work to you as a developing artist? Did it satisfy some personal need and thereby help you to grow as a human being?

Summary of Step 16

In the final phase of work, your scene will begin to play under its own power, feeling simpler and shorter, and will be adjusted to meet the demands of your performance space. You now develop the *blocking*, which is the way the characters move within the configuration of the *groundplan*. Good blocking always springs from the relationship of the characters and the underlying action of the scene. You shape and pace the scene by clarifying its structure and practicing good cueing. You strive to keep each performance fresh and spontaneous without making it erratic. Your emotional experience is controlled and does not become an end in itself. You evaluate your work not only in terms of the response of others, but also in terms of your own long-term growth objectives.

Summary of Part Four

The most important discoveries are made during the actual rehearsal process as you explore your role with your fellow actors under the guidance of your director. It is in this day-by-day work that you begin to experience the action in specific relationship and find personal significance in your character's needs, choices, objectives, and actions. As you begin to recreate the inner process by which reaction becomes action, either automatically or through deliberation and choice, interaction by interaction, you begin to transform as a new "me," a new version of yourself, emerges. Thus the character is formed by the same process that forms your everyday personality, by your experience of actually living as if you were in the character's world, feeling the character's needs as if they were your own, making the choices he or she makes as if they were your own, and doing the things the character does to try to achieve his or her objectives in each beat, each scene, and overall as he or she strives toward a superobjective. This sequence of objectives emerges as your "map" of the role, the score that will guide and inspire you through the entire performance with good pace and economy.

In the final stages of rehearsal you shape this performance to be stageworthy and dependable. You adapt it to your stage space and develop blocking that expresses the action and relationships. You perform it with controlled spontaneity and emotional clarity so as to fulfill the dramatic function of the role. You evaluate your work by balancing your own judgment with that of others, considering always your growth as an actor, your commitment to the material, and your sense of purpose in the world you serve through your work.

Your Sense of Purpose

What is it that defines a professional? In athletics we once distinguished between professional and amateur on the basis of money: the professional was paid, while the amateur (from the Latin root *amare*, "to love") participated only for the love of the sport itself. But "professional" means much more than whether someone is paid or not.

The root of the word *professional* comes from an old French verb, *profes*, that meant "to make a solemn vow," as in joining a religious order. In our culture, professionals have special knowledge or skills that give them power over other people: doctors, lawyers, clergymen, and others of the "professional class" are expected to use their special powers only for the benefit of those they serve. Thus a professional is someone who *professes* an ethical standard. They have accepted personal responsibility for work that will affect the lives of others.

As an actor, you have special power over others. You might not take acting as seriously as that, but it is true. The great director Michael Langham once told me how he came to dedicate his life to the theater: During World War II he was a prisoner of war in a camp for British officers. As the years passed, many of the men lost heart and committed suicide. To pass the time, Michael formed a dramatic society that performed plays, and one of them was Shakespeare's *King Lear*. The morning after the show, Michael's closest friend in the barrack told him that he had decided to kill himself the previous night, but the play had given him a reason to live. As Michael put it, "I knew at that moment that this was something I wanted to do for the rest of my life."

However you find it, your sense of purpose is what will give you courage and power as an actor. It grows from your respect for your own talent, your love for the specific material you are performing, and your desire to use both to serve your audience. It is this drive to be *at service* through your art that will finally overcome the self-consciousness of your ego and carry you beyond yourself, giving you a transcendent purpose from which comes dignity, fulfillment, and ongoing artistic vitality.

Stanislavski called this ongoing artistic vitality "theatrical youthfulness." Near the end of his life he addressed a group of young actors with these words:

> The first essential to retain a youthful performance is to keep the idea of the play alive. That is why the dramatist wrote it and that is why you decided to produce it. One should not be on the stage, one should not put on a play for the sake of acting

or producing only. Yes, you must be excited about your profession. You must love it devotedly and passionately, but not for itself, not for its laurels, not for the pleasure and delight it brings to you as artists. You must love your chosen profession because it gives you the opportunity to communicate ideas that are important and necessary to your audience. Because it gives you the opportunity, through the ideas that you dramatize on the stage and through your characterizations, to educate your audience and to make them better, finer, wiser, and more useful members of society.[1]

The art of acting has always had a very special service to render, one that has become increasingly important today. It is rooted in the actor's ability to transform, to become "someone else." At a time when many of us feel more and more insignificant and impotent, the actor's ability to be "in charge" of personal reality can be a source of hope and inspiration to us. Just as a play may teach us something about who we are, the actor's ability to transform may teach us something about who we may *become*. Acting can be a celebration of our power to control our own destiny. When we realize this, we find a renewed sense of ethical and spiritual purpose that is a source of great energy and courage.

---

[1] Nikolai Gorchakov, *Stanislavski Directs* (New York: Funk & Wagnalls, 1954), pp. 40–41.

APPENDIX A

A Sample Television Scene

From *Cheers* by Tom Reeder[1]

[Carla works as a waitress in the Cheers bar, which is managed by Diane. In this scene, Carla has just received an offer of marriage from Ben Ludlow, an eminent psychologist she has been dating. She has reacted strangely to the proposal and has gone into the back room to think. Diane follows her to see what's wrong.]

[Int. pool room. Carla is standing lost in thought. Diane enters.]

DIANE: Carla, I couldn't help noticing that you're not exactly leaping for joy. Bennett Ludlow is a wonderful catch.

CARLA *[WITH DIFFICULTY]:* There are things he doesn't know about me.

DIANE: A little mystery is good for a marriage. What haven't you told him?

CARLA: Well, I haven't been completely honest about my kids.

DIANE: What haven't you told him about them?

CARLA: That they live.

DIANE: He doesn't know you have children?

CARLA: Shhhhh!

DIANE: Carla, you have to tell him. He's going to wonder who those little people are running around the house.

CARLA: I'm hoping he'll be too polite to ask.

[Off Diane's Look.]

CARLA *(CONT'D):* I didn't want to scare him off.

DIANE: Seriously, Carla, it's only fair that you tell him immediately that you have five children.

CARLA: Six.

DIANE: Okay, six. But if you wait, if you put this off—I thought it was five?

CARLA: It was. But I just came from the doctor.

[Diane groans with recognition.]

DIANE: Carla, when you took hygiene in high school, did you cut the "how-not-to" lecture?

CARLA: I had to. I was pregnant. I tell you I'm the most fertile woman who ever lived. For me there's only one method of birth control that's absolutely foolproof, but it makes me sick to my stomach.

DIANE: What's that?

CARLA: Saying no.

[Ludlow enters.]

LUDLOW: Carla, are you all right?

DIANE: Well, I'm going to go celebrate with the others. We're like a big family here at Cheers. You know what they say about a big family— more to love. I always say—

CARLA: Beat it.

DIANE: Bye.

[Diane exits.]

LUDLOW: Carla, my proposal wasn't received with the enthusiasm I expected it to be. In fact, it occurred to me that I never actually heard you say "yes."

CARLA: I know. Benny, I have to tell you some things about myself.

LUDLOW: This sounds serious.

CARLA: It is. Benny, have you ever seen "The Brady Bunch"?

LUDLOW: Yes, I think so.

CARLA: Picture them with knives.

LUDLOW: I don't understand.

CARLA: I have five children.

LUDLOW: Five?

CARLA: Well . . . five and counting. You're going to be a daddy.

[Ludlow sits down.]

LUDLOW: This is quite a day.

CARLA: You now have my permission to withdraw the proposal.

LUDLOW: Do you want me to withdraw the proposal, Carla?

CARLA: I want you to do what you want to do.

LUDLOW: I want to marry you.

CARLA: You're kidding. Wow. What class.

LUDLOW: I still haven't heard you say yes.

CARLA: I know. *[Genuinely puzzled]* Why do you think that is?

LUDLOW: I think if you examine your feelings, you'll know.

CARLA: Yeah, I guess I know. I love somebody else.

LUDLOW: Who?

CARLA: I don't know his name. I haven't met him yet, but I've had this real clear picture of him in my mind for what seems like forever. He's going to walk into this bar some night. Actually, not walk. More like swagger. You know, confident but not cocky. He's okay-looking, but he's no pretty boy. He's a swell dresser. He's wearing this burgundy leather jacket. His nose is broken in all the right places. He's got this scar on his chin he won't talk about. He cracks his knuckles all the time. Drives me up the wall, but, what can you do? Doesn't talk much. Doesn't have to. He falls for me hard. I hurt him a few times. He gets over it. We get married.

[She turns to Ludlow.]

CARLA *(CONT'D):*   So you see, it would be kind of messy if I was already married when he gets here.

LUDLOW: You know something, Carla? I sort of have a dream girl myself.

CARLA: What's she like?

LUDLOW: She's a spunky, hearty, little curly-haired spitfire, who doesn't know what's good for her.

CARLA: I hope you find her some day.

LUDLOW: Me too. And I want you to know I intend to take care of this child financially.

CARLA: You bet your buns you will, Benny Baby.

[He exits. Carla stands there considering her fate.]

Suggested Plays and Anthologies

Plays

The following American plays are good sources of scenes with the qualities most useful for this book. Most of them are available in inexpensive paperback "acting editions" from the publishers indicated.

After the Fall by Arthur Miller (Dramatists Play Service)

Ah, Wilderness! by Eugene O'Neill (Samuel French)

All My Sons by Arthur Miller (Dramatists Play Service)

The Amen Corner by James Baldwin (Samuel French)

American Buffalo by David Mamet (Samuel French)

The Andersonville Trial by Saul Levitt (Dramatists Play Service)

And Miss Reardon Drinks a Little by Paul Zindel (Dramatists Play Service)

Angels in America by Tony Kushner (Theatre Communications Group)

Anna Christie by Eugene O'Neill (Vintage Books)

Bedrooms: Five Comedies by Renee Taylor and Joseph Bologna (Samuel French)

Bent by Martin Sherman (Samuel French)

Birdbath by Leonard Melfi (Samuel French)

Born Yesterday by Garson Kanin (Dramatists Play Service)

Cat on a Hot Tin Roof by Tennessee Williams (Dramatists Play Service)

Chapter Two by Neil Simon (Samuel French)

The Chase by Horton Foote (Dramatists Play Service)

The Children's Hour by Lillian Hellman (Dramatists Play Service)

The Colored Museum by George C. Wolfe (Broadway Play Publishing)

Come Back, Little Sheba by William Inge (Samuel French)

Come Back to the 5 & Dime, Jimmy Dean, Jimmy Dean by Ed Graczyk (Samuel French)

A Coupla White Chicks Sitting Around Talking by John Ford Noonan (Samuel French)

Crimes of the Heart by Beth Henley (Dramatists Play Service)

Crossing Delancey by Susan Sandler (Samuel French)

The Crucible by Arthur Miller (Dramatists Play Service)

The Dark at the Top of the Stairs by William Inge (Dramatists Play Service)

A Day in the Death of Joe Egg by Peter Nichols (Samuel French)

Death of a Salesman by Arthur Miller (Dramatists Play Service)

The Death of Bessie Smith by Edward Albee (Plume)

A Delicate Balance by Edward Albee (Samuel French)

Division Street by Steve Tesich (Samuel French)

Duet for One by Tom Kempinski (Samuel French)

The Eccentricities of a Nightingale by Tennessee Williams (Dramatists Play Service)

Effect of Gamma Rays on Man-in-the-Moon Marigolds by Paul Zindel (Bantam)

Enter Laughing by Joseph Stein (Samuel French)

Extremities by William Mastrosimone (Samuel French)

Fences by August Wilson (Samuel French)

Fool for Love by Sam Shepard (Dramatists Play Service)

Frankie and Johnny in the Clair de Lune by Terrence McNally (Dramatists Play Service)

The Gingerbread Lady by Neil Simon (Samuel French)

The Glass Menagerie by Tennessee Williams (Dramatists Play Service)

Glengarry Glen Ross by David Mamet (Samuel French)

Golden Boy by Clifford Odets (Dramatists Play Service)

A Hatful of Rain by Michael Vincente Gazzo (Samuel French)

The Heidi Chronicles by Wendy Wasserstein (Dramatists Play Service)

The House of Blue Leaves by John Guare (Samuel French)

The Immigrant by Mark Harelik (Broadway Play Publishing)

I Never Sang for My Father by Robert Anderson (Dramatists Play Service)

I Ought to Be in Pictures by Neil Simon (Samuel French)

It Had to Be You by Renee Taylor and Joseph Bologna (Samuel French)

Last of the Red Hot Lovers by Neil Simon (Samuel French)

Last Summer at Bluefish Cove by Jane Chambers (JH Press)

Laundry and Bourbon by James McLure (Dramatists Play Service)

A Lie of the Mind by Sam Shepard (Dramatists Play Service)

The Little Foxes by Lillian Hellman (Dramatists Play Service)

Long Day's Journey into Night by Eugene O'Neill (Yale University Press)

Look Homeward, Angel by Ketti Frings (Samuel French)

Lost in Yonkers by Neil Simon (Samuel French)

Lovers and Other Strangers by Renee Taylor and Joseph Bologna (Samuel French)

Luv by Murray Schisgal (Dramatists Play Service)

The Matchmaker by Thornton Wilder (Samuel French)

The Middle Ages by A. R. Gurney, Jr. (Dramatists Play Service)

Moonchildren by Michael Weller (Samuel French)

A Moon for the Misbegotten by Eugene O'Neill (Samuel French)

Murder at the Howard Johnson's by Ron Clark and Sam Bobrick (Samuel French)

The Nerd by Larry Shue (Dramatists Play Service)

'Night, Mother by Marsha Norman (Dramatists Play Service)

The Night of the Iguana by Tennessee Williams (Dramatists Play Service)

No Place to Be Somebody by Charles Gordone (Samuel French)

The Odd Couple (Female Version) by Neil Simon (Samuel French)

The Odd Couple (Male Version) by Neil Simon (Samuel French)

Of Mice and Men by John Steinbeck (Dramatists Play Service)

Oh Dad, Poor Dad, Mamma's Hung You in the Closet and I'm Feelin' So Sad by Arthur Kopit (Samuel French)

The Only Game in Town by Frank D. Gilroy (Samuel French)

On the Open Road by Steve Tesich (Samuel French)

The Philadelphia Story by Philip Barry (Samuel French)

Picnic by William Inge (Dramatists Play Service)

The Prisoner of Second Avenue by Neil Simon (Samuel French)

The Rainmaker by N. Richard Nash (Samuel French)

A Raisin in the Sun by Lorraine Hansberry (Samuel French)

The Red Coat by John Patrick Shanley (Dramatists Play Service)

Scenes from American Life by A. R. Gurney, Jr. (Samuel French)

The Sea Horse by Edward J. Moore (Samuel French)

Sexual Perversity in Chicago by David Mamet (Samuel French)

The Shadow Box by Michael Cristofer (Samuel French)

The Sign in Sidney Brustein's Window by Lorraine Hansberry (Samuel French)

Six Degrees of Separation by John Guare (Dramatists Play Service)

Speed-the-Plow by David Mamet (Samuel French)

Splendor in the Grass by William Inge (Dramatists Play Service)

Spoils of War by Michael Weller (Samuel French)

Steel Magnolias by Robert Harling (Dramatists Play Service)

Strange Snow by Stephen Metcalfe (Samuel French)

A Streetcar Named Desire by Tennessee Williams (Dramatists Play Service)

The Subject Was Roses by Frank D. Gilroy (Samuel French)

Summer and Smoke by Tennessee Williams (Dramatists Play Service)

Sweet Bird of Youth by Tennessee Williams (Dramatists Play Service)

The Tenth Man by Paddy Chayefsky (Samuel French)

That Championship Season by Jason Miller (Samuel French)

The Time of Your Life by William Saroyan (Samuel French)

To Gillian on Her Thirty-Seventh Birthday by Michael Brady (Broadway Play Publishing)

A Touch of the Poet by Eugene O'Neill (Random House)

Toys in the Attic by Lillian Hellman (Dramatists Play Service)

Tribute by Bernard Slade (Samuel French)

True West by Sam Shepard (Samuel French)

Twice around the Park by Murray Schisgal (Samuel French)

A View from the Bridge by Arthur Miller (Dramatists Play Service)

Vikings by Stephen Metcalfe (Samuel French)

Waiting for Lefty by Clifford Odets (Grove Press)

What I Did Last Summer by A. R. Gurney, Jr. (Dramatists Play Service)

When You Comin' Back, Red Ryder? by Mark Medoff (Dramatists Play Service)

Who's Afraid of Virginia Woolf? by Edward Albee (Dramatists Play Service)

The Women by Clare Boothe Luce (Dramatists Play Service)

Yellowman by Dael Orlandersmith (Vintage)

The Zoo Story by Edward Albee (Dramatists Play Service)

Zoot Suit and Other Plays by Luis Valdez (Arte Publico Press)

Play and Scene Anthologies

There are a number of anthologies of scenes on the market for student actors; they can be found in specialty book stores or online. Most of these books index scenes in a variety of ways (male-male, female-male, female-female, and by genre and ethnicity). They can be useful for picking a scene, but remember that for our purposes you must also read the entire play from which the scene comes.

24 Favorite One Act Plays ed. Bennett Cerf, Van H. Cartmell (Main Street Books)

99 Film Scenes for Actors ed. Angela Nicholas (Avon)

The Actor's Book of Scenes from New Plays ed. Eric Lane (Penguin USA)

The Actor's Scenebook ed. Michael Schulman (Bantam Books)

The Best American Short Plays 1997–1998 ed. Glenn Young (Applause Theatre Books)

The Best American Short Plays 1999–2000 ed. Glenn Young (Applause Theatre Books)

The Best American Short Plays 2000–2001 ed. Mark Glubke (Applause Theatre Books)

Duo! Best Scenes for the 90's (Applause Acting Series) ed. John Horvath, Byrna Wortman, Lavonne Mueller, Jack Temchin (Applause Theatre Books)

Duo! Best Scenes of the 90's ed. John Horvath (Applause Theatre Books)

Famous American Plays of the 70's (The Laurel Drama Series) ed. Ted Hoffman (Laurel)

Five Comic One-Act Plays by Anton Chekhov (Dover Thrift Editions)

Great Scenes and Monologues for Actors ed. Eva Mekler, Michael Schulman (St. Martin's Press)

Great Scenes and Monologues for Actors ed. Michael Schulman (St. Martin's Press)

One Act Plays for Acting Students: An Anthology of Short One-Act Plays for One, Two, or Three Actors ed. Norman Bert (Meriwether)

Plays for Young Audiences: An Anthology of Selected Plays for Young Audiences ed. Max Bush, Roger Ellis (Meriwether)

Plays from the Contemporary American Theatre ed. Brooks McNamara (Signet)

The Scenebook for Actors ed. Norman A. Bert (Meriwether)

Scenes and Monologs from the Best New Plays ed. Roger Ellis (Meriwether)

The Ultimate Scene and Monologue Source Book by Ed Hooks (Backstage Books)

Wordplays 5: An Anthology of New American Drama: Plays by James Strahs, James Lapine-Stephen Sondheim, Des McAnuff, John Jesurun, Kathy Acker (PAJ)

Wordplays: An Anthology of New American Drama by Maria Fornes, Ronald Tavel, Jean-Claude Van Itallie, William Hauptman (Farrar, Straus, and Giroux)

Anthologies for Students of Color

Asian American Drama: 9 Plays from the Multiethnic Landscape ed. Brian Nelson (Applause Theatre Books)

Beyond the Pale: Dramatic Writing from First Nations Writers & Writers of Color ed. Yvette Nolan (Consortium Books)

Black Comedy: Nine Plays ed. Pamela Faith Jackson, Karimah (Applause Theatre Books)

Black Drama in America: An Anthology ed. Darwin T. Turner (Howard University Press)

Black Theatre USA Revised and Expanded Edition, Vol. 1: Plays by African Americans From 1847 to Today ed. James V. Hatch, Ted Shine (Free Press)

Black Thunder: An Anthology of Contemporary African American Drama ed. William B. Branch (Signet)

Colored Contradictions: An Anthology of Contemporary African-American Plays ed. Robert Alexander, Harry Justin Elam (Plume Books)

Contemporary Armenian American Drama: An Anthology ed. Nishan Parlakian, S. Peter Cowe (Columbia University Press)

Contemporary Plays by Women of Color ed. Kathy A. Perkins (Routledge)

Drama for a New South Africa: Seven Plays ed. David Graver (Indiana University Press)

The Fire This Time: African American Plays for the 21st Century ed. Robert Alexander, Harry Justin Elam (Theatre Communications Group)

Great Scenes from Minority Playwrights: Seventy-Four Scenes of Cultural Diversity ed. Marsh Cassady (Meriwether)

Latin American Theatre in Translation: An Anthology of Works from Mexico, the Caribbean and the Southern Cone ed. Charles Philip Thomas, Marco Antonio de la Parra (Xlibris)

Moon Marked and Touched by Sun: Plays by African-American Women ed. Sydne Mahone (Theatre Communications Group)

Multicultural Theatre II: Contemporary Hispanic, Asian and African-American Plays ed. Roger Ellis (Meriwether)

The National Black Drama Anthology: Eleven Plays from America's Leading African-American Theaters ed. Woodie King, Jr. (Applause Theatre Books)

Playwrights of Color ed. Meg Swanson, Robin Murray (Intercultural Press)

Political Stages: A Dramatic Anthology ed. Emily Mann, David Roessel (Applause Theatre Books)

Seven Black Plays: The Theodore Ward Prize for African American Playwriting ed. Chuck Smith (Northwestern)

Seventh Generation: An Anthology of Native American Plays ed. Mimi D'Aponte (Theatre Communications Group)

Unbroken Thread: An Anthology of Plays by Asian American Women ed. Roberta Uno (University of Massachusetts Press)

Voices of Color: 50 Scenes and Monologues by African American Playwrights (Applause Acting Series) ed. Woodie King, Jr. (Applause Theatre Books)

War Plays by Women: An International Anthology ed. Claire M. Tylee, Elaine Turner, Agnes Cardinal (Routledge)

GLOSSARY OF THEATER AND FILM TERMINOLOGY

Action   Used in two ways. In a play or film script, the dramatic action is what happens in the story, scene, or beat in the most fundamental sense. For the actor, the action is what his or her character does to try to fulfill a need by winning some objective. Stanislavski spoke of both spiritual (inner) and physical (outer) action. Note that speaking is one of the most common forms of action; that is, a saying is also a doing. To be "in action" is to be totally involved in the task at hand and is the most desirable condition for the actor. Action is the most fundamental concept behind most systems of acting. (See also *Automatic action, Choice, Indirect action, Inner action, Justifying, Motivation, Objective, Reacting, Score, Stimulus, Strategy, Suppression,* and *Verb.*)

Ad lib   To insert words of your own into a script, usually on the spur of the moment.

Agent   Someone who represents and markets actors. An agent normally gets a 10 percent commission on everything an actor earns. In film and television, actors are usually auditioned only when their names are submitted by a licensed agent, so getting an agent is often the first step in initiating a professional film or television career.

The American Federation of Television and Radio Artists (AFTRA)   The union that covers radio acting and some television shows that are not filmed.

Attitude   The way your character feels about something that has happened.

Automatic action   Stanislavski's term for what we call a habit or reflex; something your character does without thinking.

Beat   A unit of action with its own specific conflict and crisis. In each beat a character has a single objective. Beats are formed of interactions and flow to create the underlying structure of a scene. The term may have been created by someone with a Russian accent saying "bit" of action, though it makes sense as a unit of rhythm (as in "downbeat") because the flow of the beats is the primary rhythm of a scene.

Beat change   When one of the characters changes a strategy or objective, moving the scene in a new direction. A beat change results from either an automatic action or a deliberate choice made by one of the characters.

Believability   Something consistent with the created reality and style of the world of the story and the personality of the character, whether like everyday life or not.

Bio   (See *Résumé.*)

Blocking   Establishing the positions and movements of the characters on the stage or in relation to the camera. Good blocking should express the underlying action of the scene. (See also *Mark.*)

Breakdown   (See *Scenario.*)

Call   The time an actor is to report for work. Missing a call is a serious offense. In the theater, calls are posted on the call board; in film and television, they are announced on a call sheet distributed near the end of each day's shooting for the following day.

Callback   There are usually preliminary auditions in the audition process from which a small number of actors are called back for a final audition.

Casting director   Preliminary auditions, especially in film and television, are usually conducted by a casting director who then selects the actors for callbacks with the director or producer. Casting directors are extremely important to actors starting out; they can be more important to the establishment of a career than are agents.

Cheating out   Standing so that your face is turned slightly toward the audience or camera. Cheating out is more important on stage than in film.

Choice   When pursuing a need, your character may consider several alternative courses of action and then make a strategic choice that appears to hold out the best chance of success. By examining your character's significant choices, you can gain a wealth of information about them.

Climax   The "main event," which is the resolution of the underlying conflict of a story and therefore ends the suspense. Scenes normally do not have climaxes, because the suspense of the story must carry into the next scene.

Continuity   In film and television, making sure that every detail of a shot matches the shots that precede or follow it. An actor has to be aware, for instance, of whether his or her right hand was over the left, how much liquid was in the glass, and so on. Continuity is the responsibility of the script supervisor, an unsung hero who remembers details like these even days later.

Costume parade   The first showing of the costumes on the set and under lights for approval by the director.

Coverage   In film, a scene is often shot from a wide perspective called the *master;* the camera is then repositioned for tighter shots called *coverage,* which the editor will later insert into the master. Consequently the actor's performance in coverage must match that of the master. Also the *close-ups,* which are the most demanding on the actors, are shot hours after the master, and actors must be careful to "save" something for them.

Crisis   The event in a story after which the outcome becomes, in hindsight, inevitable. Before this point, the energy of the story rises in suspense; during the crisis, the outcome hangs in the balance; and after the crisis, the energy flows toward resolution. While a crisis (or *turning point*) leads to a climax, it is not always the same thing as the climax and is often not the emotional high point of the story. A scene has a crisis in which the main issue of that scene is decided. A beat also has a crisis just before the beat change.

Cross   When the actor moves from point A to point B. Such movements need to be justified by some inner need. There are different kinds of crosses, such as the "banana," which is a slight curve so that the actor ends cheated out.

Cue   Anything that causes something to happen. For the actor it refers to the line or event just before his or her character speaks or moves. It can also refer to one change in lighting or sound.

Cueing   The way in which one line follows another. In real life we often overlap one another in speech and begin responding slightly before the other person has finished speaking. In film, overlapping is sometimes avoided because it limits the editor's ability to cut from take to take. ("Cueing" also means helping actors learn or remember lines by prompting them, as in "Will you cue me?")

Cue-to-cue   A form of technical rehearsal in which the actors are asked to jump from light cue to light cue.

Demonstration   Bertolt Brecht's idea that the actor does not "become" the character completely, but rather "demonstrates" the character's behavior for the audience while still expressing some attitude about it. Although this may sound like "indicating," the good Brechtian actor's passionate commitment to the ethical point being made gives the performance its own special kind of reality, while ordinary indicating feels merely empty and unreal.

Denouement   French for "unraveling"; that final portion of a story in which the loose ends are wrapped up.

Deputy   In an Equity company, a member of the cast elected to serve as the representative of the actors to the management. (See also *Equity.*)

Downstage   At one time, stages were sloped to enhance the illusion of perspective, so when heading toward the audience, actors were literally moving "down" stage, and when backing away from the audience, actors were literally moving "up" stage. Even though our stages today are rarely sloped (or "raked"), we still use this terminology.

Dramatic   When the outcome of an event is important and cannot be foretold, we say it is *dramatic.* The essence is in wondering "What will happen?" (See also *Suspense.*)

Dramatic function   The job a character was created to do within the story. Can be related to plot, meaning, our understanding of the main character, or any combination of these.

Dress rehearsal   The final rehearsals that are conducted under performance conditions.

Dual consciousness   The actor's ability to be immersed in the character and the character's world, while still reserving a level of awareness for artistic judgment. Different types of material make different demands on actors; film requires the virtual elimination of the actor's awareness in favor of the character's.

Economy   Doing enough to fulfill the dramatic function and believability of the character but avoiding extraneous details or effort.

Emotion memory (or Recall)   The actor's application of a memory from his or her real or imaginary past to enrich his or her response to the situation in the scene. While this device may be useful in rehearsal, it should never be used in performance for fear of taking the actor out of the here and now.

Empathy   The actor's ability to put himself or herself in the place of another person, both for purposes of observation and for applying the Magic If to a role. It is possible to empathize with someone even if we do not sympathize with them.

Equity   The Actors Equity Association (AEA), the main theatrical union for actors. *The Equity Rule Book* establishes the conditions under which actors may work in the theater. Grievances are reported to the elected Equity deputy.

Exposition   Providing information about what has happened before in order to help the audience understand what is going on in a story or scene. The difficulty in writing or playing exposition lies in not interrupting the action by falling into an "informational" tone. One old piece of advice is to "make exposition ammunition"; that is, your character must have a reason for providing expository information, and it must be justified by inner need.

Extra A nonspeaking actor who rounds out the reality of a scene. Professional extras in film are skilled workers who can repeat precise movements and blocking and know how to be believable without being distracting.

Eye line In film, the direction in which you are looking must match the spatial relationship established by the camera in the scene. Usually the other actor will stand in a spot that will give you the correct eye line. When your eye line is "close to the lens" the other actor may be pressed up against the camera. The Director of Photography (DP) or the camera operator will guide you in providing the correct eye line.

Focus Whatever you are concentrating on at any given moment, usually your objective.

Functional traits Those traits that a character was given (or that you provide) to allow the character to believably fulfill his or her dramatic function in the story.

Givens More completely, the Given Circumstances; the world and situation within which your character lives, especially as they affect his or her action. The circumstances include who, when, and where.

Going up Forgetting your lines. Although a terrible experience, forgetting your lines can sometimes provide wonderfully rich moments if you keep your action going, perhaps even resorting to paraphrase. Lines are learned more tenuously in film than on stage to guarantee the kind of freshness and authenticity the camera demands.

Head shot The glossy 8 × 10 photograph an actor hands out along with his or her résumé. The photograph should be attractive but not limiting in the way it portrays you—its function is merely to help someone remember you.

Improvisation Performing without a script. While most comedic improvs are based on a scenario in which the actors have some idea of the basic beats of the scene and the climax, an "open-ended" improv may be based only on a situation or relationship. In traditional theater, some directors use improvisation as a rehearsal device in which the actors explore their characters in situations beyond those contained in the script. Many good actors are terrible at improvisation, and many good improvisers are better at stand-up comedy than at characterizational acting.

Indicating Showing instead of doing; that is, standing outside the reality of your character and playing the emotion or some quality of the character instead of immersing yourself in the experience of the action.

Indirect action When some obstacle impedes direct action, a character may choose an indirect strategy, saying or doing one thing while really intending another. The obstacle may be internal or external. When there is indirect action, there is also subtext. (See also *Subtext*.)

Inner action The inner process of reaction, attitude, need, and choice that results in outer or observable action. A believable performance integrates inner and outer action into one flow of stimulus and response. This integration is called *justifying* the external action by connecting it to an internal process.

Inner monologue The "stream of consciousness" of the character. As a training or rehearsal device, actors sometimes verbalize or at least think through their characters' inner monologues to be sure they have provided full inner justification for their external actions.

Intention   (See *Objective.*)

Interaction   One give and take between the characters, sometimes also called a *moment*. Each interaction can be judged by asking two questions: First, has one character truly affected the other? Second, does this "link" in the chain of action and reaction move the scene in the proper direction?

Justifying   The process of connecting outer (visible or audible) actions to inner needs and processes. The script provides the basis for the outer actions; however much the script may also hint at the inner action which produces this outer action, it is ultimately the task of the actor to justify. In justifying, the actor puts his or her personal stamp on the performance.

The League of Resident Theatres (LORT)   An organization that has negotiated a specific contract with Actors Equity governing the operation of regional theaters that maintain a resident company. Being a member of a resident company, including the various summer festivals, is the best growth experience an actor can have and is the traditional stepping stone from training to a professional career.

Magic If   Stanislavski's technique in which you put yourself in the given circumstances of your character *as if* you live in that world, then experience your character's needs *as if* they are your own, and finally choose and pursue your character's action *as if* it were your own. This process results in metamorphosis or transformation, whereby the actor "becomes" the character, though without losing the dual consciousness that provides artistic control. (See also *Transformation.*)

Mark   In film and television, a piece of colored tape that shows the actor where to stand at a specific moment in a scene. The actor must "hit" each mark without looking down.

Master   (See *Coverage.*)

Matching   In film, the need to match details and emotional tone from shot to shot. (See also *Coverage.*)

Metamorphosis   (See *Transformation.*)

Moment   A brief period of time when something of special value is happening. We speak of "making the moment." Can also refer to one interaction between characters. Several interactions make up a beat.

Motivation   The inner need that drives your character's action, which usually comes from something that has just happened in the scene, however much it may awaken some long-standing need in your character. It is important that the energy coming from this past motivation drives you toward some objective in the immediate future because you can't play motivation, only the action toward which it drives you. In other words, *motivation must lead to aspiration.*

Need   Whatever your character needs that drives him or her to pursue an action to try to satisfy that need.

Objective   The goal your character pursues through action to satisfy a need. An objective is best defined using a transitive verb phrase, such as "to persuade him to give me a territory in town." In practice, the most useful form of objective is *a change in the* *other character*, such as "to get him to look at me with compassion." The terms *intention* and *task* are sometimes used to mean *objective*.

Off book   Memorizing your lines so that you can perform without the script. During the period immediately after going off book, it is expected that you will need prompting; call for lines without apology so that you do not lose concentration or your sense of action.

Out (or In)   On stage, away from center (or toward center).

Pace   The momentum or flow of a scene. Pace is different from tempo, which refers to the speed of the action. Regardless of tempo, a scene has good pace when the connections of cause and effect, action and reaction are strong and real so that the action flows with integrity and purpose. Paradoxically, sometimes slowing the tempo of a scene improves the pace because the actors are forced to experience the connections of action and reaction more fully.

Paraphrase   To use your own words in place of the words of the script, though with an effort to mean the same thing. Paraphrasing can sometimes help you to examine the meaning of your lines and to "own" or personalize them. It can also help carry you over moments in which you "go up" on your lines. In film and television, a modest amount of paraphrase is sometimes tolerated as a way of producing a more personal performance.

Personalization   The indispensable process of making the character's needs, choices, habits, and actions your own. (See also *Magic If*.)

Playable   What we call an objective or action that is useful in performance and contributes to the movement of the scene. The most playable objectives are SIP: singular, immediate, and personally important. The best way of defining an objective is as *a change in the other character*, as this will draw your energy outward and into the immediate future, bringing you into strong interaction with the other character.

Playing through   Letting the action flow with good pace by keeping your awareness moving toward the future objective and avoiding falling into internal feelings or the past. Your energy is most useful to the scene when it is oriented *outward and toward the future*.

Plot   The sequence of events as the story unfolds. The actor needs to be aware of how each of his or her actions moves the plot forward and especially when a scene contains a *plot point* that must be solidly established.

Projection   In the theater, speaking loudly enough and with enough clarity to be heard and understood throughout the auditorium. Good projection is usually more a matter of clarity than of sheer volume. In film, however, any sense of projection will read as unreal. When Michael Redgrave, already an accomplished stage actor, did his first take for a camera, he asked the director how it was. The director, who was standing behind the camera, said, "It was fine, Michael, except I could hear you."

Prompt book   The copy of the script kept by the stage manager that contains the blocking, the lighting and sound cues, and all the rest of the physical aspects of a production. It is possible to recreate a production from the prompt book, as is sometimes done in the case of great European productions. Some of Shakespeare's plays were printed from his prompt books. In film, the script supervisor records every shot in a book, permitting the editor to access particular takes in a scene.

Prompting   Giving actors lines when they ask for them. Actors usually call out, "Line." Lines are given by the stage manager in the theater and by the script supervisor in film.

Prop   Anything your character handles. It is wise to begin working with rehearsal substitutes as soon as you are off book.

Public solitude   Stanislavski's concept of how actors, by focusing on their objectives, can "forget" that they are in public and thereby avoid self-consciousness and stage fright. The concept does *not* imply that actors neglect the discipline of producing a publicly effective performance.

Reacting   Allowing yourself to respond to the immediate stimulus in the scene and allowing that stimulus to make you do what your character does in response. This requires real hearing and seeing and the courage to surrender yourself to accepting the stimulus as your partner actually provides it, rather than playing what you have previously created in your head. Because everything your character does is in reaction to something, we say that "acting is reacting." The ideal is to be "more moved than moving."

Read-through   A rehearsal in which the entire scene or script is read aloud.

Reel   A videotape containing a compilation of an actor's appearances on film. A reel may contain work in student films or classroom exercises. Although a reel may be useful in the early stages of a career, it is rarely worth the effort expended on making it.

Relationship   All characters exist in relationship to other characters, and we come to understand characters mostly by observing the way others relate to them. For this reason we say that actors create each other's characters more than they create their own. It is important to develop your character in specific relationship to the performances of the other actors in your scene.

Relaxation   The key to most everything in acting. For the actor, relaxation is not a reduction of energy but rather a freeing of energy and a readiness to react. The term *restful alertness* is the best description.

Repertory   A company of actors that performs a body of plays. When a number of plays are performed on alternating days, it is called *rotating* or true repertory. The regional repertory movement in this country is an important source of entry-level jobs for young actors.

Résumé   A listing of an actor's experience, showing the roles he or she has performed, including where and under whose direction, as well as training and special skills.

Running lines   Two or more actors going over their lines together. The best way to memorize lines.

Scenario   A listing of the beats of a scene. Also called a breakdown, the scenario gives the actors a sense of the underlying structure of the scene; it serves as a sort of map as they move through the journey of the scene.

Scene   A section of a play that has its own main conflict and crisis. A scene usually contains one of the major events of the story and makes a major change in the plot or central relationship. In a film or television script, scenes are also determined by changes in location or lighting requirements, and each scene is given a "slug line" as in INTERIOR LIVING ROOM—NIGHT. In some older plays, scenes are marked by the entrance of major characters; these are called *French scenes*.

Score   Stanislavski spoke of the score of a role as the sequence of objectives. The actor comes to understand the logic of this sequence, and eventually this flow of action carries the actor through the role, serving as a kind of total choreography for mind and body. (See also *Spine*.)

The Screen Actors Guild (SAG)   The main union for film and television shot on film. A powerful union with over 100,000 members, 94 percent of whom are unemployed at any given moment. An aspiring actor can join the union by being hired for a union job, though this is a catch-22. Some agents represent young actors informally even before they are members of the union, thereby giving them a chance to audition for union jobs.

Sense memory (or Recall*)*   The use of a memory from the actor's real or imagined past of sensations similar to those required by a scene so as to enrich the actor's response to the scene. Stanislavski believed that every cell in the body is capable of such memory and urged actors to develop their storehouse of such memories.

Set up   To prepare for the punch line of a joke, the entrance of a character, or some other important event. In television sitcoms, setting up a joke is called "laying pipe." In film, a set-up is one camera position.

Shot   In film or television, one piece of film from one camera position, beginning when the director calls "action" and ending when he or she calls "cut."

Sides   Sides were small versions of a play that contained only the speeches of individual characters; these are rarely used now. In film, sides are miniature copies of the scenes to be shot on a given day and are distributed each morning by the second assistant director.

Spine   Stanislavski spoke of each beat and scene in a role fitting together like the vertebrae in a spine. When the actor experiences this connectedness, the role begins to flow as if under its own power. Also called the *through-line* of the role. Similar to the score of the role, in which the through-line is understood as a sequence of objectives.

Spiritual action   Stanislavski's term for the inner phase of action, which produces physical or external action.

Spontaneity   Each moment of a performance should feel as if it were happening for the first time and yet be controllable and consistent from performance to performance. Stanislavski believed that this can be achieved by an act being so fully rehearsed that it becomes "automatic and therefore free"; that is, because you don't need to think about it, you are free to experience it afresh each time you do it.

Stage directions   The indications in a script about the character's gestures, tone of voice, and so on, such as (*he moves away angrily*). Some teachers and directors tell actors to ignore stage directions because in some so-called acting versions of a play they may have been inserted not by the writer but from the prompt book of an earlier production. However, many writers provide stage directions, and you should consider them for the information they contain about the behavior and emotion of your character, even if that behavior eventually takes a different form in your particular production.

Stage fright   Everyone gets it. The only antidote is to be fully focused on the task at hand and passionately committed to it.

Stage right or left   Directions on a stage are given from the actor's point of view as he or she faces the audience; that is, stage right is audience left. In film, the director will say either "Move to your right," or "Move to camera left."

Stimulus   The thing your character is reacting to at any given moment. The most useful stimuli are in the immediate present, however much they may trigger needs or feelings from your character's past.

Strategy   Your character's sense of how best to pursue an objective within the given circumstances. The strategic choices the character makes express the way he or she sees the world and the other characters.

Substitution   A special kind of emotional recall in which someone from the actor's real or imaginary past is substituted (in the actor's mind) for the other character in a scene to enrich the actor's response to that character. This is a dangerous device because it may take the actor out of the here and now, but with caution it may be useful.

Subtext   When pursuing an objective indirectly, your character may be saying or doing one thing while really meaning another. In such cases there is a difference between the surface activity (the text) and the hidden agenda (the subtext). The character may be conscious or unconscious of the subtext; in either case it is important that the actor avoid bringing the subtext to the surface of the scene by trying to play or indicate it.

Superobjective   The character's main desire in life; the life goal toward which each of his or her objectives is directed. Characters, like people in everyday life, are often unconscious of this life goal, but it pervades everything they do.

Suppression   The choice *not* to act in response to a stimulus, but rather to "hold down" the energy the stimulus has aroused. By allowing yourself to feel the urge to act and then making the effort to suppress it, you can turn a "not doing" into a playable action. A "not doing" is useful because it helps to build suspense.

Suspense   A condition in which something is about to happen but the outcome is delayed and in doubt. The more important the potential event, the more doubtful the outcome, and the longer it is delayed, the greater the suspense. The essence is the question, "What will happen?" which, from the actor's point of view, usually translates into "What will he or she choose to do?"

Table reading   Usually the first rehearsal of a script in which the actors sit at a table and read it aloud. During any reading, it is important that the actors try to play in relationship and experience the action of the scene and not fall into a flat, "literary" tone.

Take   In film, a single shot from "action" to "cut." There may be many takes of a given shot until the director is satisfied. The take intended for use will be indicated by the director saying, "Print it," though several takes may be printed to give the editor a choice of performances.

Task   (See *Objective*.)

Technical rehearsal   In theater the rehearsal in which the lighting, sound, and nearly completed set are first brought together under the command of the stage manager. At the technical rehearsal, the lighting and sound board operators have their first chance to rehearse their cues, and the designers are seeing the set and props in action. Great patience is required of the actors at a "tech" rehearsal, which is sometimes quite lengthy.

Tempo   The speed at which a scene is played; not to be confused with pace. The actor must be able to justify the action at any tempo; Stanislavski would sometimes have actors play a scene at various tempos as a training exercise. Within a given tempo, there are variations that produce rhythm.

Temporhythm   The term used by Stanislavski to refer to the whole issue of overall tempo and the variations in tempo that produce the rhythms within a scene. He believed that the temporhythms of a scene are fundamental to the correctness of the action of the scene and "all by themselves" can move the actor to the correct emotion.

Through-line   (See *Spine.*)

Transaction   (See *Interaction.*)

Transformation   The process by which the actor begins to "become" the character or, more accurately, make the character his or her "own." To use the language of William James, the character becomes a new "me" to be inhabited by the actor's "I." Stanislavski used the term *metamorphosis.*

Universal   The quality of an action, event, or character trait that allows everyone to recognize and respond to it as related to their own lives.

Upstage   (See *Downstage.*)

Upstaging   In theater, literally to position yourself upstage of the other character so that he or she is forced to turn toward you (and away from the audience) to speak to you. In film or theater this term also refers to any behavior that draws attention to you and away from the other character. To be avoided.

Verb   The verb phrase that succinctly describes your action at a given moment, such as "to persuade." Only transitive verbs are used, and all forms of the verb "to be" (such as "being angry" or "being a victim") are avoided.

Visualization   The actor's ability to imagine a situation, to "see" it in the mind's eye. A special and effective form of rehearsal called Visuo-Motor Behavior Rehearsal (VMBR) allows you to visualize your performance while in a relaxed state, allowing your deep muscles to respond to your mental image.

INDEX

It is recommended that readers check headings in the Table of Contents for items not found below.